A COMPLETE LAB MANUAL FOR BIOTECHNOLOGY

DR. NOBLE K KURIAN

Made with ♥ on the Notion Press Platform
www.notionpress.com

Dedicating to all my students who made me a real teacher

Contents

Contents

Preface

This book is a comprehensive practical hand book for UG as well as PG students of Biotechnology. The book is designed in the format mostly followed in most colleges of India. So the students can directly copy the experiments to their record books. As all experiments are proved to be conducted succesfully in small college labs, it will be 100% useful to the students. Mainly this book focusses on experiments on Molecular Biology as well as Genetic engineering. Immunology is also a part of the book including ELISA, antigen-antibody tests, blood grouping, blood smear prepartion etc. Another highlight of this book is the inclusion environmental biotechnology protocols. Most of the environmental biotechnology protocols have been included in the book. The main advantage of buying this book is that it contain protocols for excercises for research methodology for biologist which is researched and developed by the author itself. This include how to write review, houw to file patent, how to apply for research projects etc. These all peculiarities makes this book unique. Experience the it in the pages beyond..

Acknowledgements

Acknowledging all the Universities and colleges wich had given chance for me to try and retry and optimise these protocols which helped to present these protocols in the most perfect way before you..

Prologue

The book starts with how to prepare solutions for laboratory experiments. Then next part will be of environmental biotechnology. Total of thirteen experiments are listed this section. Folowed by molecular biology and genetic engineering section which is composed of four experiments. Then the book contains Immunology experiments composed of five experiments followed by Research methodology for biologist of four experiments. A total of 27 experiments are published in this book

CHAPTER ONE

Preparation of Solutions

Aim

To prepare solutions for Biotechnology experiments

Molar solutions

Molar solutions were prepared by dissolving gram molecular weight of the solute making one litre of solution. It means to prepare 1 litre solution, we have to dissolve solute equal to the molecular weight of the solute in grams

Normal solutions

The normal solution is defined as the gram equivalent weight per liter of the solution (solvent).

Normal solution = gram equivalent weight of solute/liter of the solution (solvent) = Eq.wt/L.

These solutions are expressed as N.

Gram equivalent weight = Gram molecular weight/valency.

Example of Gram equivalent weight e.g NaCl

NaCl gram molecular weight = 58.5 g

Valency =1

58.5/1 = 58.5 gram equivalent weight.

To make a 1 N sodium chloride solution

The molecular weight of NaCl is 58.5.

Gram equivalent weight of NaCl = molecular weight/1 (valency).

So dissolve 58.5 grams of NaCl in distilled water and makeup to one liter.

Dissolve 58.5 grams of NaCl in distilled water to make one liter.

Percentage Solutions

This is per hundred part of the total solution.

There are three possibilities for a percent solution.

Weight/weight:

It is a percentage of solute in 100 grams of final solution equal to solute + solvent.

e.g .For the 5% solution take 5 grams of NaCl dissolved in 95 grams of water which is around 95 mL.

Weight/volume:

5 grams of NaCl dissolved in water and the volume is made 100 ml is called a 5% solution of NaCl.

Volume/volume:

It is composed of two solutions. e.g. if we take 5 mL of acid and dilute it to 100 mL of water will be a 5% solution of that acid.

Dilutions

When a buffer (or any solution for that matter) is something-something X, that just means that you should dilute at that ratio. For example, if you want to make 50 mL of TAE buffer, use 1 mL of 50x stock + 49 mL of H2O (1 TAE : 50 mL total volume). You can scale that ratio up or down as needed.

Prepare 1X TAE from 50X TAE of volume of 300 mL

Use the formula C1V1=C2V2

Where, C1 = Concentration of the Stock solution

C2 = Concentration of Working solution

V = Volume

If we follow the formula

50X * X = 1X * 300ml (X=Volume)

= 6ml of 50X stock TAE

Now use 6ml of 50X TAE and make up the volume till 300ml with Deionized water

CHAPTER TWO

Dissolved Oxygen (DO) Estimation

AIM: To estimate the amount of Dissolved Oxygen (DO) present in given water sample.

INTRODUCTION:

Dissolved oxygen (DO) levels in natural and wastewaters depend on the physical, chemical and biochemical activities in the water body. The analysis of DO is a key test in water pollution and waste treatment process control. DO levels of up to 8 ppm is normal and will support aquatic life. DO of 6 ppm will result in development in mosquito larvae and proliferation of soil bacteria.

Methods for the estimation of DO:

(1) lodometric method

(2) Membrane electrode method

(3) Azide modification method

(4) Permanganate method

(5) Alum flocculation method

(6) CuSO4 – Sulfuric acid ``modified'' method.

lodometric method:

PRINCIPLE:

Iodometric test is most precise and reliable titrimetric procedure for DO analysis. The method is based on addition of divalent manganese ions in the solution, followed by addition of strong alkali iodide azide solution to sample present in the glass stoppered bottle. DO present in dilution water rapidly oxidizes an equivalent amount of dispersed divalent manganese hydroxide [Mn(OH)2] precipitate to the hydroxide of the higher valance. [Mn(OH)3]. Thus Mn++ is oxidized to Mn+++. In presence of iodine ions in acidic solution, oxidized manganese (Mn+++) reverts to divalent state

(Mn++) with liberation of Iodine (12) equivalent to original DO content. Iodine is then titrated against standard thiosulfate solution, using starch as an indicator.

REAGENTS:

1. MnSO4 solution: Dissolve 480 g MnSO4 4H2O or 400 g MnSO4 2H2O or 364 g MnSO4H2O in distilled water and dilute to 1 L. The MNSO4 solution should not give a colour with starch when added to a acidified potassium iodide (KI) solution.

2. Alkali-iodide-azide reagent: Dissolve 500 g NaOH (or 700 gm KOH), 135 g NaI (or 150 gm KI), dissolve in distilled water and dilute to 1 L. Add 10 g NaN3 in 40 ml distilled water and mix with earlier solution. Potassium and sodium salts may be used interchangeably. These reagents should not give a color with starch solution when diluted and acidified.

3. Concentrated sulphuric acid solution:

4. 2% starch solution

5. Standard sodium thiosulphate titrant: 6.205 g Na2S2O2 5H2O in distilled water and add 1.5 mL 6N NaOH or 0.4 g solid NaOH and dilute to 1 L.

PROCEDURE:

1. Collect the sample in BOD bottle having capacity of 300 mL.
2. In this bottle add 1 mL MnSO4 solution followed by addition of 1 mL Alkali iodide azide reagent.

NOTE: If pipettes are dipped into sample, rinse then before returning them to reagent bottles. Alternatively, hold pipette tips just above liquid surface when adding reagents.

3. Stopper the bottle carefully to exclude air bubble and mix by inverting bottle a few times.
4. When precipitate has settled sufficiently (approximately half the bottle volume) to leave clear supernatant above the manganese hydroxide floc.
5. Add 1 mL concentrated H2SO4.
6. Restopper the bottle and mix it thoroughly to completely dissolve the precipitates.
7. Take 200 mL of this mixture from bottle to flask.
8. Add 1 mL 2% starch solution as indicator.
9. Titrate it with 0.025 M Na2S2O3 solution.
10. Record the end point, when the blue colour of starch disappears.

CALCULATION:

For titration of 200 mL sample, 1 mL 0.025 M $Na_2S_2O_3$ = 1 mg DO per Litre.

CHAPTER THREE

Biochemical Oxygen Demand (BOD)

AIM: To estimate Biochemical Oxygen Demand (BOD) in the given water sample.

INTRODUCTION:

Definition: Biochemical Oxygen Demand can be defined as amount of oxygen required (consumed) by nonphotosynthetic microorganisms for the oxidation of organic compounds in dark at 20oC.

The biochemical oxygen demand (BOD) determination is an empirical test in which standardized laboratory procedures are used to determine the relative oxygen requirements of wastewaters, effluents and polluted waters. The test has its widest application in measuring waste loadings to treatment plants and in evaluating the BOD – removal efficiency of such treatment systems. The test measures the molecular oxygen utilized during a specified incubation period for the biochemical degradation of organic material (carbonaceous demand) and oxygen used to oxidize inorganic material such as sulfides and ferrous iron. It also measure the amount of oxygen used to oxidize reduced form of nitrogen (nitrogenous demand) unless an inhibitor prevents their oxidation. The seeding & dilution procedures provide an estimate of BOD at pH 6.5-7.5.

Dilution Requirement: The BOD concentration in most waste waters exceeds the concentration of dissolved oxygen (DO) available in a saturated sample. Therefore, it is necessary to dilute the sample before incubation to bring the oxygen demand and supply into appropriate balance. Because the bacterial growth requires nutrients such as nitrogen, phosphorous and trace metals, this are added to dilution water, which is buffered to ensure that the pH of incubated sample remain in range suitable for bacterial growth. Complete stabilization of a sample may require a period of incubation too long for practical purposes; therefore, 5-days have been accepted as a standard incubation period.

There are two types of method generally used to estimate BOD.

1] 5-day BOD test (by Azide modification method)

2] Ultimate BOD test [UBOD]

Here we will follow the 5-Day BOD test.

5-DAY BOD TEST

PRINCIPLE:

The method consists of filling with sample, to overflowing an airtight bottle of the specified size and incubating it at the specified temperature for 5 days. Dissolved oxygen is measured initially and after incubation and the BOD is computed from the difference between initial and final DO. Because the initial DO is determined immediately after the dilution is made, all oxygen uptake including that occurring during the first 15 min is included in the BOD measurement. DO measurement is being done with the help of azide modification method.

REQUIREMENTS:

1. BOD bottles : capacity 300 mL
2. BOD incubator

REAGENTS:

***1. Phosphate buffer solution.* (pH: 7.2):** Dissolve 8.5 gm KH_2PO_4, 21.75 gm K_2HPO_4, 33.4 gm $Na_2HPO_4.7H_2O$ and 1.7 gm NH_4Cl in about 500 ml distilled water and dilute to 1 litre. The pH should be 7.2 without further adjustments. Alternatively, dissolve 42.5 gm KH_2PO_4 or 54.3 gm K_2HPO_4 in about 700 ml of distilled water. Adjust pH to 7.2 with 30% NaOH and dilute to 1 litre.

2. Magnesium sulfate solution: Dissolve 22.5 g $MgSO_4. 7H_2O$ in distilled water and dilute to 1 L.

3. Calcium chloride solution: Dissolve 27.5 g $CaCl_2$ in distilled water and dilute to 1 L

4. Ferric chloride solution: Dissolve 0.25 g $FeCl_3. 6H_2O$ in distilled water and dilute to 1 L.

5. Sodium sulphite solution: Dissolve 1.575 g Na_2SO_3 in 1000 mL distilled water. This solution is not stable, prepare daily.

6. Glucose-Glutamic acid solution: Dry reagent grade glucose and reagent grade Glutamic acid at 103°C for 1 h. Add 150 mg glucose and 150 mg Glutamic acid to distilled water and dilute to 1 L. Prepare fresh immediately before use.

PROCEDURE:

A] PREPARATION OF DILUTION WATER:

Placed desired volume of water in a suitable bottle and add 1mL each of phosphate buffer, $MgSO_4$, $CaCl_2$, $FeCl_3$ solution per litre of water. Seed solution water if desired. For seeding add a population of microorganisms. The perfect seed is effluent from a biological treatment system, processing the waste. Where this is not available, use the supernatant from domestic wastewater after settling at room temperature for at least 1h. Before use bring dilution water temperature to 20°C. Saturate with DO by shaking in a partially filled bottle or by aerating with organic free filtered air. Alternatively, store in cotton plugged bottles long enough for water to become saturated with DO. Protect water quality by using clean glassware's, tubing and bottles.

Periodically check dilution water quality, seed effective ness and analytical technique by making BOD measurement on glucose-gluconic acid solution. This is 'standard' check solution.

B] PREPARATION OF BOD BOTTLES

1. Filter the sample of sewage of other wastewater sample to remove large pieces of suspended matter.
2. Take four BOD bottles, having capacity of 300 mL.
3. Label them as blank, 1:100, 1:50, 1:33.
4. Add 3 mL, 6 mL, and 9 mL of the sample in to the bottle labelled as 1:100, 1:50 and 1:33 respectively, in blank do not add sample.
5. Now fill each bottle with dilution water by over flowing it.
6. Seal each bottle by placing lid on every of it.
7. Immediately at 0 h measure the DO of the blank
8. Refill the blank and put in its original condition
9. Keep all the bottles at temperature 20±1°C, in dark for 5 days.

C] MEASUREMENT OF RESIDUAL OXYGEN

1. After 5 days, take out all bottles from incubator.
2. Measure the DO of the blank bottle and sample bottle, by azide modification method.
3. Put the DO values in following formula and calculate the BOD for the given sample.,

CALCULATION:

BOD mg / L = A-B x dilution factor

where,

A = DO of the diluted sample immediately after preparation, mg/L

B = DO of the diluted sample after 5 days of incubation mg/L

CHAPTER FOUR

Estimation of Chemical Oxygen Demand (COD)

AIM: Estimation of Chemical Oxygen Demand (COD) in given water sample.

INTRODUCTION:

Definition: The Chemical oxygen demand is a measure of oxygen required by strong chemical oxidants for the oxidation of organic matter present in the sample.

For sample from a specific source, COD can be related empirically to BOD, organic carbon, or organic matter. The test is useful for monitoring and control after correlation has been established. The dichromate reflux method is preferred over procedures using other oxidants because of superior oxidizing ability, applicability to a wide variety of samples, and ease of manipulation. Oxidation of most organic compounds is 95 to 100% of the theoretical value. Pyridine and related compounds is resistant to oxidation and volatile organic compounds are oxidized only to the extent that they remain in contact with the oxidant. Ammonia present either in the waste or liberated from nitrogen containing organic matter is not oxidized in the absence of significant concentration of free chloride ions.

TYPES OF METHOD:

There are basically two types of method are available for the estimation of COD.

1. Open reflux method
2. Close reflux method

Open reflux method is suitable for a wide range of wastes where a large sample size is preferred. Here we will follow the open reflux method.

OPEN REFLUX METHOD

PRINCIPLE:

The method of COD which uses dichromate as oxidant which is carrying out oxidation by heating under reflux condition .A boiling mixture of chromic and sulphuric acids oxidizes most types of organic matter in presence of silver sulfate (Ag2SO4 as a catalyst). A sample is refluxed in strongly acid solution with a known excess of potassium dichromate (K2Cr2O7). After digestion, the remaining unreduced K2Cr2O7 is titrated with ferrous ammonium sulfate adding few drops of ferroin indicator to determine the amount of K2Cr2O7 consumed and utilizable organic matter is calculated in terms of oxygen equivalent. The titration reaction corresponds to the oxidation of FAS by dichromate. When all dichromate is reduced (FAS act as a reducing agent) after that ferroin indicator is reduced, which indicate endpoint of titration process. Colour change: Brilliant Green to Reddish Brown

REQUIREMENTS:

1. APPARATUS: COD digestion apparatus

2. REAGENTS:

a. ***Standard potassium dichromate solution (0.0417 M):*** Dissolve 12.259 g K2Cr2O7, primary standard grade, previously dried at 103°C for 2 h, in distilled water and dilute to 1000 mL.

b. ***Sulfuric acid reagent:*** Add Ag2SO4, reagent of technical grade crystals or powder to concentrated H2SO4 at the rate of 5.5 g Ag2SO4/Kg H2SO4. Let stand 1 to 2 day to dissolve Ag2SO4.

c. ***Ferroin indicator solution:*** Dissolve 1.485 g 1,10-phenanthroline monohydrate and 695 mg FeSO4.7H2O in distilled water and dilute to 100 mL. This indicator solution may be purchased already prepared.

d. ***Standard ferrous ammonium sulfate (FAS) titrant (approx. 0.25M):*** Dissolve 98 g Fe(NH4)2(SO4)2. 6H2O in distilled water. Add 20 ml concentrated H2SO4 cool, and dilute to 1000 mL. Standardize this solution daily against standard K2Cr2O7 solution.

PROCEDURE:

1. Take 25 mL water sample in the digestion tube.
2. Prepare blank by taking 25 mL of distilled water instead of sample.
3. Add 12.5 mL of 0.0417 M K2Cr2O7 and mix it properly
4. Add 37.5 mL of H2SO4 solution.
5. Put the tubes in COD digestion apparatus. Connect them with condenser.
6. Allow it to be digested and refluxed at 160°C for 2 h.
7. Cool it and take the content of tube in to flask

8. Add 1.5 ml ferroin indicator solution.

9. Titrate the content of the flask with 0.025 M Ferrous Ammonium Sulfate solution (FAS)

10. Note down the titration reading for blank and sample tube

11. Use following equation and calculate the amount of COD for the given sample.

CALCULATION:

(A – B) x M x 8000

COD as mg O2/L =

mL of sample

where, A = mL of FAS used for blank

B = mL of FAS used for sample

M = Molarity of FAS

8000 = milliequivalent weight of Oxygen x 1000 mL/L

CHAPTER FIVE

Water Hardness Estimation

AIM: To estimate the hardness of the given water sample

INTRODUCTION:

Originally water hardness was understood to be a measure of a capacity of water to precipitate soap. Soap is precipitated chiefly by calcium and magnesium ions present in water sample. Calcium and magnesium often are in complex form. Frequently present with organic constituent and it is difficult to define their role in water hardness. Nowadays total hardness is defined as the sum of calcium and magnesium concentration both expressed as calcium carbonate in mg/L.

The hardness may range from 0 to 100 mg/L depending on the source and treatment to which the water has been subjected.

METHOD:

At present two methods are available for the estimation of water hardness.

1. Estimation of hardness by calcium
2. EDTA titrimetric method.

Here we will follow: **EDTA TITRIMETRIC METHOD**

EDTA TITRIMETRIC METHOD

PRINCIPLE:

Ethylene Diamine Tetra acetic acid (EDTA) and its sodium salts (abbreviated EDTA) form a chelated soluble complex when added to a solution of certain metal cations. If a small amount of dye such as Eriochrome Black – T or Calmagite is added to an aqueous solution containing calcium and magnesium ion at a pH of 10+/-0.1, the solution becomes wine red. If EDTA is added as titrant the calcium and magnesium will be complexed. When all of the magnesium and calcium ions have been complexed the solution turns from wine red to blue, which is the end point of the titration. Magnesium ions must be present to yield satisfactory end points. The sharpness of endpoints increases with increase in pH. However, the pH cannot be increased indefinitely because of the danger of precipitating calcium carbonate or magnesium hydroxide.

REAGENTS:

1. *Buffer solution:* Dissolve 16.9 gm NH4Cl in 143 ml concentrated ammonium hydroxide (NH4OH) solution. Add 1.25 gm magnesium salt of EDTA (available commercially) dilute to 250 ml with distilled water. If the magnesium salt of EDTA is unavailable, dissolve 1.179 gm disodium salt of EDTA dehydrate (analytical grade reagents) and 780 mg magnesium sulfate (MgSO4 .7H2O) or 644 mg magnesium chloride (MgCL2.6H2O) in 50 ml distilled water. Add this solution to 16.9 gm ammonium chloride and 143 ml conc. NH4SO4 with mixing and dilute to 250 ml with distilled water.

Store this solution in a plastic or glass container for no longer than 1 month. Stopper tightly to prevent the loss of ammonia or uptake of CO2. Discard buffer, when 1 or 2 ml added to the sample fails to produce a pH of 10 +/- 0.1 at the titration end point.

2. *Indicator:* Eriochrome Black – T [1-(1-hydroxy –2-naphthyl-azo) –5-nitro-s-napthol-4-sulfonic acid] No. 203 in the colour index.

Dissolve 0.5 gm dye in 100ml 2-methoxy methanol (also called Ethylene glycol monomethyl ether) or triethanol amine. Add 2 drops per 50 ml solution to be titrated.

Calmagite: This is stable in aqueous solution and produces the same colour change as Eriochrome Black-T with a sharper end point. Dissolve 0.1 gm calmagite in 100 ml distilled water. Use 1 ml per 50 ml solution to be titrated.

3. *Standard EDTA titrant (0.01M):* Weigh 3.723 gm sodium salt of EDTA, dissolve in distilled water and dilute to 1000 ml.

PROCEDURE:

1. Take 25 ml of water sample dilute it up to 50 ml with distilled water.
2. Add 1-2 ml buffer solution
3. Usually 1 ml will be sufficient to give a pH of 10 – 10.1
4. Add 1.2 drops of indicator solution (Eriochrome Black T), wine red color will be developed.
5. Titrate the mixture with standard EDTA titrant, slowly with continuous stirring (shaking) until the last reddish tinge disappears.
6. Complete the titration within 5 min.
7. At the end point the solution is normally blue.

CALCULATION:

Hardness (EDTA) A x B x 10000
(as mg $CaCO_3$ per litre) =
ml of sample (25 ml)
Where,
A = ml of titrant for sample
B = mg $CaCO_3$ equivalent to 1ml EDTA titrant (i.e. 1 mg)

CHAPTER SIX

PHOSPHORUS PHOSPHATE ESTIMATION

AIM: To estimate the Phosphorous phosphate present in given water sample.

INTRODUCTION:

Phosphorous occurs in natural water and in wastewaters mostly as phosphates. These are classified as... (1) Orthophosphates (2) Condensed phosphates or Polyphosphates and (3) Organically bound phosphates. They occur in solutions, in particles or in the bodies of aquatic organism. These forms of phosphates arise from a variety of sources. Orthophosphates applied to agricultural or residential cultivated land as fertilizers are carried out into surface water with storm run-off. Polyphosphates are mainly present in detergents. Organic phosphates are formed primarily by biological processes for e.g. from the body wastes and food residues. Phosphorous is essential to the growth of organism. It can be the nutrient that limits the primary productivity of a water body. Phosphorous stimulate the growth of photosynthetic aquatic microorganisms and other microorganisms.

METHODS:

Phosphorous analyses embody two general steps:

a. Conversion of phosphorous form of interest to dissolved orthophosphates

b. Colorimetric determination of dissolved orthophosphates.

ASCORBIC ACID METHOD

PRINCIPLE:

Ammonium molybdate and potassium antimonyl tartrate react in acid medium with orthophosphate to form a heteropoly acid- phosphomolybdic acid that is reduced to intensely coloured molybdenum blue by ascorbic acid. Ascorbic acid may be used as a reducing agent which reduces ammonium phosphomolybdic acid to intensely blue coloured complex of molybdenum blue that is proportional to the amount of phosphate present.

REQUIREMENTS:

1. Spectrophotometers
2. Acid washed glasswares

REAGENTS:

1. 5 N Sulphuric acid (H2SO4): Dilute 70 ml concentrate H2SO4 up to 500 ml with distilled water.

2. Potassium antimonyl tartrate solution:

Dissolve 1.375gm K(SbO)C4H4O6½H2O in 400ml distilled water. Dilute it up to 500 ml with distilled water.

3. Ammonium molybdate solution: Dissolve 20gm [(NH4)6 Mo7O24.4H2O] in 500ml distilled water.

4. Ascorbic acid solution (0.1M): Dissolve 1.76 gm ascorbic acid in 100ml distilled water. Store at 4 °C. The solution is stable for 1 week.

5. Combine reagent: Mix the above reagent in the following proportion:

50 ml 5 N H2SO4

+ 5 ml Potassium antimonyl tartrate solution

+ 15 ml Ammonium molybdate solution

+ 30 ml Ascorbic acid solution

100 ml (combined reagent)

If the turbidity forms in the combined reagent shake and let it stand for few minutes until turbidity disappears before proceeding. The reagent is stable for 4 hours.

6. Stock phosphate solution:

Dissolve 219.5 mg anhydrous KH2PO4 in 1000ml distilled water. [1ml = 50 μg phosphate- phosphorous]

7. Standard phosphate solution:

Dilute 50 ml stock phosphate solution in 1000ml-distilled water.

[1ml = 2.5 μg phosphate-phosphorous]

PROCEDURE:

1. Take different aliquots of standard phosphate solution, from 1.0, 2.0,.... 5.0 ml.
2. In blank don't add standard phosphate solution.
3. Take different aliquots of unknown sample like 1.0., 3.0 and 5.0 ml
4. Add the distilled water in all the tubes to make the final volume 10.0 ml.

5. Add 1.6 ml combined reagent in all the tubes

6. Incubate all the tubes at room temperature for 15 min.

7. Take O.D. of all the tubes at 880nm

8. Prepare a standard curve by plotting absorbance reading of standards against phosphate concentrations of standards.

9. By comparing sample absorbance with the standard curve find out the concentration of phosphate present in the given unknown sample of water.

10. Note down the result and give your conclusion.

CHAPTER SEVEN

Chloride Estimation

AIM: Estimation of Chloride in Water Sample

INTRODUCTION:

Chloride in the form of chloride ion (Cl-) is one of the major inorganic anions in water and wastewater. In potable water, the salty taste produced by chloride concentration is variable and dependent on the chemical composition of water. Some waters containing 250 mg Cl- per litre may have a detectable salty taste, if the cation is sodium. On the other hand, the typical salty taste may be absent in water containing as much as 1000mg Cl- per litre, when the predominant cations are calcium and magnesium. The chloride concentration is higher in wastewater than in raw water because sodium chloride (NaCl) is a common matter of diet and passes unchanged through system. Along the seacoast, chloride may be present in high concentration because of leakage of salt water into the sewage system. Industrial processes also may increase chloride. High chloride content may harm metallic pipes and structures and growing plants.

Selection of the method:

There are five different methods available for the estimation of chloride:

1. Argentometric method
2. Mercuric nitrate method
3. Potentiometric method
4. Automated – ferricyanide method
5. Ion chromatographic method

Here we will estimate the chloride as per Argentometric method.

PRINCIPLE:

In a neutral or slightly alkaline solution, potassium chromate can indicate the end point of the silver nitrate titration of chloride. Silver chloride is precipitated quantitatively before red silver chromate is formed.

REACTION:

NaCl + AgNO3 ---------AgCl2 (white ppt.) + NaNO3

K2CrO4 + AgNO3--------- KNO3+Ag2CrO4 (Silver Chromate)

REAGENTS:

1. ***Potassium chromate indicator solution (K2CrO4):*** Dissolve 50 gm K2CrO4 in a little distilled water. Add AgNO3 solution until a definite red precipitate is formed. Let it stand for 12 hours, filter and dilute it to 1 litre with distilled water.

2. ***Standard silver nitrate titrant (0.0141M):*** Dissolve 2.395 gm AgNO3 in distilled water and dilute to 1000ml. Standardize against 0.0141 M NaCl. Store in brown bottle.

3. ***Standard NaCl (0.0141M):*** Dissolve 824.0 mg of NaCl (dried at 140oC) in distilled water and dilute to 1000 ml. (1ml = 500 ug Cl-)

PROCEDURE:

Sample Preparation:

Take 100 ml of sample in 250 ml conical flask. If chlorine is higher in the sample, dilute the sample and then take 100 ml of diluted sample. If the sample is highly coloured add 3ml Al(OH)3 suspension, mix, let settle and filter.

Titration:

1. Set the pH of the sample in the range of 7 – 10 with the help of H2SO4 or NaOH.
2. Add 1ml K2CrO4 indicator solution.
3. Titrate it with standard AgNO3 titrant to a pinkish yellow end point.
4. Be consistent in end point recognition.

CALCULATION:

mg Cl- / L = (A – B) x N x 35450/ ml of sample (100ml)

where,

A = ml titration for sample

B = ml titration for blank

C = Normality of AgNO3 (0.0141 N)

2] mg NaCl/L = (mg Cl-/L) x 1.65

CHAPTER EIGHT

Determination of TS, TDS and TSS in Water

Aim of the experiment:

To determine Total Solids (TS), Total Dissolved Solids (TDS), Total Suspended Solids (TSS), Volatile Suspended Solids (VSS) and Fixed Suspended Solids (FSS) in the given water sample.

Theory:

Water contains different types of impurities like suspended, colloidal and dissolved materials in it. Based on its contaminants water can be broadly defined as mixture of different types of solids in a liquid base. Solids may be classified as settleable, suspended, dissolved, volatile and fixed. All these types together called as **total solids.** The settleable solids are those, which are capable of settling when, placed in a quiescent condition. The suspended solids are those which are not soluble in water and remain in suspension for a long period. These solids impart turbidity to the water. The dissolved solids impart colour and odour to water. The total, settleable, suspended and dissolved solids include volatile and fixed components.

Solids form an important component in treatment processes. The suspended and settleable solids have to be removed in the sedimentation units and the dissolved solids will have to be removed in the filtration and other secondary treatment facilities. The volatile solids play an important role in biological treatment of waste water. Solids refer to matter suspended or dissolved in the water or wastewater and may affect water or effluent quality in adverse ways. Waters with high dissolved solids have poor palatability and may cause unfavourable physiological reactions in transient consumers. Solids analyses are critical for controlling biological and physical wastewater treatment processes as well as determining compliance with regulatory agency limits.

Total Dissolved Solid (TDS) is the amount of combined contents of all inorganic and organic substances contained in a liquid in molecular, ionized or micro-granular suspended form. Total dissolved solids are usually discussed only for freshwater systems, as salinity includes some of the ions constituting the definition of TDS.

Total Suspended Solids (TSS) are solids that can be trapped using a filter in water. TSS can include a wide variation in material, such as silt, decaying plant and animal matter, industrial wastes, and sewage. High concentrations of suspended solids can cause several problems to stream health and aquatic life.

Total Solids (TS) can be found by summation of **TSS** and **TDS.**

Volatile Suspended Solids (VSS)Fixed Suspended Solids (FSS) are the suspended solids associated with volatile fraction. are the suspended solids associated with the mineral fraction.

Procedure

TESTING OF SAMPLE FOR TOTAL DISSOLVED SOLIDS

To measure total dissolved solids, take a clean porcelain dish which has been washed and dried in a hot air oven at 180oC for one hour.

- Now weigh the empty evaporating dish in analytical balance. Let's denote the weight measured as W1 = 35.4329 g.
- Mix sample well and pour into a funnel with filter paper. Filter approximately 80 -100 mL of sample.
- Using pipette transfer 75mL of filtered sample in the porcelain dish.
- Switch on the oven and allowed to reach 105°C. Check and regulate oven and furnace temperatures frequently to maintain the desired temperature range.
- Place it in the hot air oven and care should be taken to prevent splattering of sample during evaporation or boiling.
- Dry the sample to get constant mass. Drying for long duration usually 1 to 2 hours is done to eliminate necessity of checking for constant mass.
- Cool the container in a desiccator. Desiccators are designed to provide an environment of standard dryness. This is maintained by the desiccant found inside. Don't leave the lid off for prolonged periods or the desiccant will soon be exhausted. Keep desiccator cover greased with the appropriate type of lubricant in order to seal the desiccator and prevent moisture from entering the desiccator as the test glassware cools.
- We should weigh the dish as soon as it has cooled to avoid absorption of moisture due to its hygroscopic nature. Samples need to be measured

accurately, weighed carefully, and dried and cooled completely.

- Note the weight with residue as W2 = 35.4498 g.

TESTING OF SAMPLE FOR TOTAL SUSPENDED SOLIDS

- Place filtration apparatus with weighed filter in filter flask.
- Mix sample well and pour into a graduated cylinder to the selected volume.
- Apply suction to filter flask and seat filter with a small amount of distilled water.
- Pour selected volume into filtration apparatus.
- Draw sample through filter into filter flask.
- Rinse graduated cylinder into filtration apparatus with three successive 10 mL portions of distilled water, allowing complete drainage between each rinsing.
- Continue suction for three minutes after filtration of final rinse is completed.
- Dry filter in an oven at 103-105°C for at least 1 hour.
- Cool filter in desiccator to room temperature.
- When cool, weigh the filter and support.

Calculation

W1 = 35. 4329 g

W2 = 35. 4498 g

V = 50. 0 mL

Weight of residue (g) W = W2 - W1 = 35. 4498 - 35. 4329 = 0. 0169 g

Weight of residue in mg (To convert W (g) to W (mg), multiply W (g) with 1000) W (mg) = 0.0169 x 1000 = 16.9mg

Multiply the weight of the dry solids (in mg) by 1,000 mL/L to convert the sample size from mL to L.

Total Dissolved Solids (mg/L)

V = Volume of the sample (mL) (To convert mL to L, multiply by 1000)

=16.9 mg/50 mL = 0.338 mg/mL

= 0.338 mg/mL x 1,000 mL/L = **338 mg/L**

W1 = 1.6329g

W2 = 1.6531g

V = 100.0 mL

Weight of residue (g) W = W2 - W1

= 1.6531 - 1.6329

= 0. 0202 g

Weight of residue in mg (To convert W (g) to W (mg), multiply W (g) with 1000)

W (mg) = 0.0202 x 1000

= 20.2 mg

Multiply the weight of the dry solids (in mg) by 1,000 mL/L to convert the sample size from mL to L.

Total Suspended Solids (mg/L)

V = Volume of the sample (mL) (To convert mL to L, multiply by 1000)

=20.2 mg/100 mL = 0.202 mg/mL

= 0.202 mg/mL x 1,000 mL/L = **202 mg/L**

Water can be classified by the amount of TDS per litre:

- fresh water < 1500 mg/L TDS

brackish water 1500 to 5000 mg/L TDS

saline water >5000 mg/L TDS

CHAPTER NINE

Ammonia Nitrogen (NH4-N) Estimation

AIM: Estimation of Ammonia-Nitrogen in given water sample by Phenate Method.

INTRODUCTION:

In waters and wastewaters, the forms of nitrogen of greatest interest are, in order of decreasing oxidation state, nitrate, nitrite, ammonia and organic nitrogen. All these forms of nitrogen, as well as nitrogen gas (N2), are biochemically interconvertible and are components of the nitrogen cycle. They are of interest for many reasons.

Ammonia is present naturally in surface and wastewaters. Its concentration generally is low in groundwater because it adsorbs to soil particles and clays and is not leached readily from soils. It is produced largely by deamination of organic nitrogen containing compounds and by hydrolysis of urea. At some water treatment plants ammonia is added to react with chlorine to form mono and dichloramine. Ammonia concentration encountered in water varies from less than 10ug ammonia-nitrogen/L in some natural surface and ground waters to more than 30 mg/L in some wastewaters.

PRINCIPLE:

Phenate method is a standard colorimetric procedure for ammonia. It involves addition of an alkaline phenol solution together with hypochlorite. The sodium nitroprusside catalyses the reaction involving phenol, hypochlorite and ammonia, to produce indophenol which has intense blue colour. The intensity of blue coloured compound is measured at 640 nm with a path length of 1 cm.

REAGENTS:

1. ***Phenol solution:*** Mix 11.1 ml liquefied phenol (>89%) with 95% v/v ethyl alcohol to a final volume of 100ml. (prepare weekly).

2. ***Sodium nitroprusside:*** (0.5% w/v) Dissolve 0.5gm sodium nitroprusside in 100ml deionized water. (Store in a bottle up to 1 month).

3. ***Alkaline citrate:*** Dissolve 200gm trisodium citrate and 10gm sodium hydroxide in deionized water. Dilute to 1L.

4. ***Sodium hypochlorite:*** About 5% available commercially.

5. ***Oxidizing solution:*** Mix 100ml alkaline citrate solution with 25ml sodium hypochlorite. Prepare fresh daily.

6. ***Stock ammonium solution:*** Dissolve 3.819gm anhydrous NH_4Cl in water and dilute 10 1L (1.00 mL = 1.00 mg N= 1.22 mg NH_3).

7. ***Standard ammonia solution:*** Use stock ammonium solution and water to prepare a calibration curve in range appropriate for the concentration of the sample.

PROCEDURE:

1. Take different aliquots of NH_4Cl standard solution from 0.1, 0.2 .....0.5 ml.
2. In blank don't add NH_4Cl.
3. Make the final volume 5.0ml with distilled water.
4. Add 0.2ml of phenol reagent in each test tube.
5. Add 0.2 ml of sodium nitroprusside solution in each tube.
6. Add 0.5ml-oxidizing solution in each tube.
7. Stopper every test tube with rubber cork.
8. Incubate all the tubes in dark at room temperature for 1 hr.
9. For unknown sample take three aliquots 0.1, 0.3, and 0.5ml and proceed in similar way as above.
10. Measures absorbance of every tube at 640nm.
11. Prepare a standard curve by plotting absorbance reading of standards against ammonia concentrations of standards.
12. By comparing sample absorbance with the standard curve, find out the concentration of ammonia present in the given unknown sample of water.
13. Note down the result and give your conclusion.

CHAPTER TEN

Nitrate Estimation

Introduction:

Nitrate is the oxidized state of nitrogen and in oxygenated surface waters, all organic and inorganic nitrogen should be in the form of nitrate. Major sources of these two forms are industrial waste waters, domestic sewage, fertilizers from run off, soil organic matter etc. It is an essential nutrient for many photosynthetic autotrophs and in some cases has been identified as the growth limiting nutrient. In quantities normally found in food or feed, nitrate becomes toxic only under condition when they reduced to nitrites, otherwise, at reasonable concentration, nitrates are rapidly excreted in the urine. As there is no direct method for nitrate estimation, the method of reducing nitrate to nitrite chemically is being used.

Two commonly employed methods are Cadmium reduction method and Overnight reduction method.

Cadmium Reduction Method:

Principle:

Nitrate in the sample is reduced quantitatively to nitrite when a sample is run through a column containing cadmium fillings loosely coated with metallic copper. The nitrite thus produced is determined by diazotizing with sulphanilamide and coupling with NNED to form a highly coloured azo dye, the extinction of which is measured at 543 nm.

Reagents:

1. Conc. Ammonium chloride solution: Dissolve 125 g of ammonium chloride in 500 ml of distilled water and store in a glass or plastic bottle.

2. Dilute ammonium chloride solution: Dilute 50 ml of conc. ammonium chloride solution to 2000 ml with distilled water and store in a glass or plastic bottle.

3. Sulphanilamide solution: Dissolve 5 g of sulphanilamide in a mixture of 50 ml of conc. HCl and about 300 ml of distilled water. Dilute to 500 ml

with water.

2. N-(1-naphthyl) – ethylene diamine dihydrochloride solution (NNED): Dissolve 0.50 g of NNED in 500 ml of distilled water. Store the solution in a dark bottle.

Experimental Procedure:

Add 1-2 ml of ammonium chloride to the 50 ml sample in the Erlenmeyer flask and mix it.

Add the sample to the column and allow it to pass through.

Collect 25 ml of the reduced solution in measuring cylinder by placing under the collection tube.

As soon as possible after reduction, add 0.50 ml of sulphanilamide and allow the reagent to react for 2 min. but not exceeding 8 minutes.

Add 0.5 ml of NNED solution and mix immediately. Between 10 minutes and 2 hrs, afterwards measure the extinction of the solution at a wavelength of 543 nm.

A correction may be made for any nitrite initially present in the sample by following the same procedure without reduction.

µg.at – NO3 – N/ltr = (Extinction x F) - C

Where, F = Dilution Factor value

C= concentration of nitrite present in the sample as µg.at – NO2 – N/ltr

CHAPTER ELEVEN

Estimation of Organic Nitrogen

Aim

To measure the amount of organic nitrogen present in the sample using Kjeldahl Method

Theory

The Kjeldahl method is used to determine the nitrogen content in organic and inorganic samples. For longer than 100 years the Kjeldahl method has been used for the determination of nitrogen in a wide range of samples. The determination of Kjeldahl nitrogen is made in foods and drinks, meat, feeds, cereals and forages for the calculation of the protein content. Also, the Kjeldahl method is used for the nitrogen determination in wastewaters, soils and other samples. The Kjeldahl procedure involves three major steps:

Digestion

The aim of the digestion procedure is to break all nitrogen bonds in the sample and convert all of the organically bonded nitrogen into ammonium ions (NH4 +). Organic carbon and hydrogen form carbon dioxide and water. In this process the organic material carbonizes which can be visualized by the transformation of the sample into black foam. During the digestion the foam decomposes and finally a clear liquid indicates the completion of the chemical reaction. For this purpose, the sample is mixed with sulfuric acid at temperatures between 350 and 380 °C. The higher the temperature used, the faster digestion can be obtained. The speed of the digestion can be greatly improved by the addition of salt and catalysts. Potassium sulfate is added in order to increase the boiling point of sulfuric acid and catalysts are added in order to increase the speed and efficiency of the digestion procedure. Oxidizing agents can also be added to improve the speed even further.

Protein (-N) + H_2SO_4 ------------à $(NH_4)_2SO_4 + CO_2 + H_2O$

After digestion is completed the sample is allowed to cool to room temperature, then diluted with water and transferred to the distillation unit.

Distillation

During the distillation step the ammonium ions (NH_4^+) are converted into ammonia (NH_3) by adding alkali (NaOH).

The ammonia (NH_3) is transferred into the receiver vessel by means of steam distillation.

$(NH_4)_2SO_4$ + 2NaOH<------à $2NH_3$ (gas) + $Na_2SO_4 + 2H_2O$

The receiving vessel for the distillate is filled with an absorbing solution in order to capture the dissolved ammonia gas. • Common absorbing solutions involve aqueous boric acid [$B(OH)_3$] of 2-4% concentration. The ammonia is quantitatively captured by the boric acid solution forming solvated ammonium ions.

$B(OH)_3 + NH_3 + H_2O$------à $NH_4^+ + B(OH)_4$

• Also, other acids can be used as precisely dosed volume of sulfuric acid or hydrochloric acid that captures the ammonia forming solvated ammonium ions.

H_2SO_4 (total) + $2NH_3$ ----------à $SO_4^{2-} + 2NH_4$

Titration

The concentration of the captured ammonium ions can be determined using two types of titrations:

• When using the boric acid solution as absorbing solution, an acid-base titration is performed using standard solutions of sulfuric acid or hydrochloric acid and a mixture of indicators. Depending on the amount of ammonium ions present, concentrations in the range of 0.01N to 0.5N are used. Alternatively, the end point can be determined potentiometrically with a pH-electrode. This titration is called direct titration.

$B(OH)_4^- + HX$-----à $X^- + B(OH)_3 + H_2O$

HX= strong acid (X= Cl^-, etc.)

• When using sulfuric acid standard solution as absorbing solution, the residual sulfuric acid (the excess not reacted with NH_3) is titrated with sodium hydroxide standard solution and by difference the amount of ammonia is calculated. This titration is called back titration.

H_2SO_4 (total) + $2NH_3$-------à $SO_4^{2-} + 2NH_4$

Procedure

The optimal sample amounts (from 0.01 to 5 g) depend on the expected nitrogen contents but also affect the choice of titrant concentration. The limit of sample amounts normally needs to be found experimentally. It should contain 30 – 140 mg N. Ideally the particle size should be < 1 mm. The sample must be homogeneous and it should be milled if necessary. The volume of sulfuric acid 98% used is a function of the expected consumption of sulfuric acid in the redox reaction converting sulfuric acid to sulfur dioxide.

Typically for 1 g sample two Kjeldahl tablets of 5 g are used together with 20 mL of 98% sulfuric acid and digestion times of 90 minutes are applied. A good ratio is 1 g of Kjeldahl catalyst mixture to 2 mL of 98% sulfuric acid. The digestion time depends on the chemical structure of the sample, the temperature, the amounts of sulfate salt and the catalyst.

As an example, in the following figures we show the processes of digestion, distillation and titration for a sample of milk.

CALCULATIONS

The calculations for % nitrogen or % protein must take into account which type of receiving solution was used and any dilution factors used during the distillation process. In the equations below, "N" represents normality. "ml blank" refers to the millilitres of base needed to back titrate a reagent blank if standard acid is the receiving solution, or refers to millilitres of standard acid needed to titrate a reagent blank if boric acid is the receiving solution.

When boric acid is used as the receiving solution the equation is:

% Nitrogen= (ml standard acid - ml blank) x N of acid x 1.4007 /weight of sample in grams

When standard acid is used as the receiving solution, the equation is:

% Nitrogen+ [(ml standard acid x N of acid) - (ml blank x N of base)] - (ml standard base x N of base) x 1.4007/ weight of sample in grams

CHAPTER TWELVE

Isolation of Nitrogen Fixing Bacteria

AIM: To isolate, cultivate and study the nitrogen fixing organisms from the given root nodule and soil samples.

INTRODUCTION:

Nitrogen fixing organisms are capable of fixing atmosphere nitrogen and convert the atmospheric gaseous nitrogen into fixed form of nitrogen that can be utilized by other microbes or plants. Mostly they convert atmospheric N2 into NH3. Thus by fixing nitrogen such microorganisms increase the soil fertility and ultimately increase the quality of crops. Hence these bacteria are used as biofertilizers. Most important group of nitrogen fixing organisms belongs to two families. 1) Azotobacteriaceae, 2) ***Rhizobiaceae.*** Other bacteria that are able to fix nitrogen are some species of ***Klebsiella*** and ***Clostridia,*** the ***Cyanobacteria*** and ***Photosynthetic*** bacteria. Various types of nitrogen fixers can be divided in to two groups.

1. Symbiotic nitrogen fixers: e.g. ***Rhizobium spp.*** They fix atmospheric nitrogen only under symbiotic condition that is when they are associated with the root nodules of leguminous plants. In these nodules these bacteria exists a pleomorphic rods (bacteroids) and other shapes.

2. Non – symbiotic nitrogen fixers: They are free-living nitrogen fixers such as ***Azotobacter spp, Azomonas spp*** and others. They do not live in symbiotic association with any other living organisms.

PRINCIPLE:

The Symbiotic and Non-symbiotic both group of nitrogen fixers can be isolated by using **NITROGEN – FREE** medium as a selective medium. This medium will selectively allow the growth of only nitrogen fixers. Because the organisms that can fix and use atmospheric nitrogen as nitrogen source and use glucose as carbon source can only grow in this medium.

[1] ISOLATION OF SYMBIOTIC NITROGEN FIXING BACTERIA: *Rhizobia*

REQUIREMENTS:

? Root nodules of leguminous plant.

? Plates of YEM (Yeast Extract Mannitol) agar,

? 1:100 diluted HgCl2,

? Forceps, glass rod, Pipettes, Test tubes, Microscope.

? Methylene blue stain,

? Reagents for Gram's staining and Capsule staining.

PROCEDURE:

1. Take a nodule from plant root by means of forceps and place it in a Petri dish having sterile distilled water.

2. Treat the nodule with 1:100 diluted HgCl2 and allow it to react for 30 seconds, and wash the nodule with sterile distilled water

3. Crush the nodule in distilled water with the help of a glass rod, prepare suspension and perform gram staining and observe the bacteroids.

4. Take a loopful of sample and streak it on YEM agar plate. Inoculate the plate at room temperature for 24- 48 hrs.

5. Observe colony characters and from an isolated colony prepare suspension and perform gram staining and capsule staining.

[2] ISOLATION OF NON- SYMBIOTIC NITROGEN FIXING BACTERIA:

Azetobacter

REQUIREMENTS:

Soil sample, Plates of Ashby's Mannitol Agar, Tubes with sterile distilled water, Pipettes, Test tubes, Methylene blue stain, Microscope, Reagents for Gram's staining and Capsule staining.

PROCEDURE:

1. Take 1gm of soil in 9 mL of sterile distilled water, shake it vigorously and allow to stand for 1 hr. Separate the supernatant.

2. Prepare the serial dilution from the soil suspension, from 10-1 to 10-3

3. From any dilution take a loopful of suspension and streak on sterile Ashby's Mannitol Agar medium.

4. Incubate the plate at room temperature for 24 to h8 hrs.

5. After incubation observe colony characters, pickup a colony and prepare suspension in distilled water.

6. From suspension of colony, prepare smears and perform Gram's staining and Capsule staining.

7. Note down the result and give your conclusion.

CHAPTER THIRTEEN

Most Probable Number (MPN) Test

Most Probable Number (MPN) is used to estimate the concentration of viable microorganisms in a sample by means of replicating liquid broth growth in ten-fold dilutions. It is commonly used in estimating microbial populations in soils, waters, and agricultural products. MPN test is particularly useful with samples that contain particulate material that interferes with plate count enumeration methods.

MPN is most commonly applied for quality testing of water i.e to ensure whether the water is safe or not in terms of bacteria present in it. A group of bacteria commonly referred to as fecal coliforms act as an indicator of fecal contamination of water. The presence of very few fecal coliform bacteria would indicate that water probably contains no disease-causing organisms, while the presence of large numbers of fecal coliform bacteria would indicate a very high probability that the water could contain disease-producing organisms making the water unsafe for consumption.

Principle

Water to be tested is diluted serially and inoculated in lactose broth, coliforms if present in water utilizes the lactose present in the medium to produce acid and gas. The presence of acid is indicated by the color change of the medium and the presence of gas is detected as gas bubbles collected in the inverted Durham tube present in the medium. The number of total coliforms is determined by counting the number of tubes giving positive reaction *(i.e both color change and gas production)* and comparing the pattern of positive results *(the number of tubes showing growth at each dilution)* with standard statistical tables.

MPN test is performed in 3 steps

1. Presumptive test
2. Confirmatory test
3. Completed test

Presumptive test

The presumptive test is a screening test to sample water for the presence of coliform organisms.

If the presumptive test is negative, no further testing is performed, and the water source is considered microbiologically safe. If, however, any tube in the series shows acid and gas, the water is considered unsafe and the confirmed test is performed on the tube displaying a positive reaction.

The method of the presumptive test varies for treated and untreated water.

Requirements

- Medium: Lactose broth or MacConkey broth or Lauryl tryptose (lactose) broth
- Glasswares: Test tubes of various capacities (20ml, 10ml, 5ml), Durham tube
- Others: Sterile pipettes

Preparation of the Medium

- Prepare medium (either MacConkey broth or lactose broth) in single and double strength concentrations.
- **For untreated or polluted water:**
    - Dispense the double strength medium in 10 tubes (10mL in each tube) and single strength medium in 5 tubes (10 mL in each tube) and add a Durham tube in an inverted position.

For treated water:

Dispense the double strength medium in 5 tubes (10mL in each tube) and 50 mL single strength medium in 1 bottle and add a Durham tube in an inverted position.

Examine the tubes to make sure that the inner vial is full of liquid with no air bubbles.

Sterilize by autoclaving at 15 lbs pressure (121°C) for 15 minutes.

Procedure of MPN test

For untreated (polluted) water

Take 10 tubes of double strength and 5 tubes of single strength for each water sample to be tested.

Using a sterile pipette add 10 mL of water to 5 tubes containing 10 mL double strength medium.

Similarly, add 1 mL of water to 5 tubes containing 10 mL double strength medium and 0.1 mL water to the remaining 5 tubes containing 10 mL single strength medium.

Incubate all the tubes at 37°C for 24 hrs. If no tubes appear positive re-incubate up to 48 hrs.

Compare the number of tubes giving a positive reaction to a standard chart and record the number of bacteria present in it.

For example, a water sample tested shows a result of 3–2–1 (3 × 10 mL positive, 2 × 1 mL positive, 1 × 0.1 mL positive) gives an MPN value of 17, i.e. the water sample contains an estimated 17 coliforms per 100 ml

Check with a standard MPN chart to get the above values

For treated (unpolluted) water

Take 1 bottle of single strength (50mL) and 5 tubes of double strength (10mL) for each water sample to be tested.

Using a sterile pipette add 50 mL of water to the bottle containing 50 mL single strength medium.

Similarly, add 10 mL of water to 5 tubes containing 10 ml double strength medium.

Incubate the tubes at 37°C for 24 hrs. If no tubes appear positive re-incubate up to 48 hrs.

Compare the number of tubes giving a positive reaction to a standard chart and record the number of bacteria present in it.

For example, a water sample tested shows a result of 1-4 (1 × 50 mL positive, 4 × 10 mL positive) gives an MPN value of 16, i.e. the water sample contains an estimated 16 coliforms per 100 mL.

Confirmatory Test

Some microorganisms other than coliforms also produce acid and gas from lactose fermentation. In order to confirm the presence of coliform, a confirmatory test is done.

From each of the fermentation tubes with positive results transfer one loopful of medium to:

3 mL lactose-broth or brilliant green lactose fermentation tube, to an agar slant and 3 mL tryptone water.

Incubate the inoculated lactose-broth fermentation tubes at 37°C and inspect gas formation after 24 ± 2 hours. If no gas production is seen, further incubate up to a maximum of 48 ±3 hours to check gas production.

The agar slants should be incubated at 37°C for 24± 2 hours and Gram-stained preparations made from the slants should be examined microscopically.

The formation of gas in lactose broth and the demonstration of Gram-negative, non-spore-forming bacilli in the corresponding agar indicates the presence of a member of the coliform group in the sample examined.

The absence of gas formation in lactose broth or the failure to demonstrate Gram-negative, non-spore-forming bacilli in the corresponding agar slant constitutes a negative test (absence of coliforms in the tested sample).

Tryptone Water Test

Incubate the tryptone water at (44.5 ±0.2°C) for 18-24 hours

Following incubation, add approximately 0.1mL of Kovacs reagent and mix gently.

The presence of indole is indicated by a red color in the Kovacs reagent, forming a film over the aqueous phase of the medium.

a. Confirmatory tests positive for indole, growth, and gas production show the presence of thermotolerant E. coli.

b. Growth and gas production in the absence of indole confirm thermotolerant coliforms.

Completed Test

Since some of the positive results from the confirmatory test may be false, it is desirable to do completed tests. For this inoculum from each positive tube of the confirmatory test is streaked on a plate of EMB or Endo agar.

In this process, a loopful of a sample from each positive BGLB tube is streaked onto selective medium like Eosin Methylene Blue agar or Endo's medium. One plate each is incubated at 37°C and another at 44.5± 0.2°C for 24 hours.

High temperature incubation (44.5 ±0.2) is for detection of thermotolerant E.coli.

Following incubation, all plates are examined for the presence of typical colonies.

Coliforms produce colonies with a greenish metallic sheen which differentiates it from non-coliform colonies (show no sheen). The presence of typical colonies on high temperature (44.5 ±0.2) indicates the presence of thermotolerant E.coli.

Advantages of MPN

Ease of interpretation, either by observation or gas emission

Sample toxins are diluted

Effective method of analyzing highly turbid samples such as sediments, sludge, mud, etc. that cannot be analyzed by membrane filtration.

Disadvantages of MPN

It takes a long time to get the results

Results are not very accurate

Requires more glassware and media

Probability of false positives

CHAPTER FOURTEEN

Slide culture of Fungus

Aim

To grow fungi by slide culture technique and identification by lactophenol staining.

Principle

Slide-culture is a rapid method of preparing fungal colonies for examination and identification with little disturbance as possible. Fungal isolates are grown directly on the slide on a thin film of agar. Identification of fungi depends largely on their macroscopic features (colony characteristics, growth rate, color, texture, diffusible pigment, exudates, aerial and submerged hyphae) and microscopic features (arrangement of spores and sporing bodies). Arrangements of conidiophores and the way in which spores are produced help in the accurate identification of filamentous fungi.

Slide culture method was first developed by Riddel in 1950 and currently, several modifications are in use. Fungi are inoculated in small blocks of potato dextrose agar medium, covered with a coverslip and incubated. After incubation, the coverslip is removed from the agar block and placed on another slide to which a dye, such as lactophenol cotton blue, may be added and observed for microscopic structures. Identification is made by microscopically examining the undisturbed sporulating structures as they were arranged during growth on the agar block under the coverslip.

Procedure

Cut a small block of a potato dextrose agar medium that has been previously poured into a culture dish to a depth of approximately 2 mm by using sterile scalpel blade or with a sterile test tube. Note: The block should be smaller than the coverslip so that it fits under.

Add the agar block to the surface of the sterile microscope slide.

With a inoculating loop, inoculate the four quadrants of the agar block with the organism and apply a sterile coverslip onto the surface of it.

Place the slide in a petriplate contained a moist filter paper or cotton, allow it to incubate at 30°C for 4-7 days.

After the incubation period, remove the coverslip and place it on a microscope slide containing a drop of lactophenol cotton or aniline blue.

Observe microscopically for the characteristic shape and arrangement of spores.

CHAPTER FIFTEEN

Isolation of genomic DNA from bacteria

Aim

To isolate genomic DNA from bacterial cells

Principle

The bacterial cell is broken down by the action of SDS and Proteinase K. The cellular components containing all macromolecules are released into the medium. Proteins and carbohydrates are removed by adding phenol-chloroform-isoamyl alcohol. Of this PCI mixture, phenol denatures the proteins while lipids and carbohydrates are removed by chloroform. Isoamyl alcohol prevents froth formation. As the impurities are removed the genomic DNA is precipitated using isopropanol / absolute ethanol from the solution. The alcohol breaks the water cage around the DNA and makes DNA precipitate out.

Procedure

Transferred 2ml bacterial overnight culture in Nutrient Broth into a micro centrifuge tube, spun for 10min. at 8000 rpm and decanted the supernatant completely.

Resuspended the pellet in 875 ml of Tris-EDTA (TE) buffer and added 5µl Proteinase K and 100µl 10% sodium dodecyl sulphate (SDS) to it.

The mixture was incubated in a water bath at 37°C for 1hr.

After incubation, added equal volume of phenol-chloroform isoamyl alcohol (25:24:1) and mixed properly until a white precipitate was seen and centrifuged at 8000 rpm for 10 minutes.

With the help of a wide mouth-cut-tip carefully collected the upper aqueous layer into a fresh tube, taking care not to carry over any phenol while pipetting.

Repeated the process twice and added an equal volume of chloroform and spun for 5min. at 8000 rpm.

Collected the upper layer into a fresh tube and added 0.1 volume sodium acetate and double volume isopropyl alcohol and spun at 8000 rpm for 10 min and decanted the supernatant.

To the pellet, added 1ml 70% ethanol and spun. Decanted the alcohol and kept the pellet for air in a covered tray.

The pellet containing the isolated DNA was then dissolved in 1 ml TE buffer 10 mM Tris (pH 7.8) and stored at -20°C for further studies.

CHAPTER SIXTEEN

Isolation of Human genomic DNA

Aim

To isolate genomic DNA from Human white blood cells

Materials required

RBC Lysis Solution

WBC Lysis Solution

Phenol- Chloroform isoamyl alcohol

Isopropanol

70% ethanol

Principle

White blood cells (WBCs) are separated from a specimen of whole human blood (or from a "buffy coat" specimen that has been separated from a whole blood sample) by mixing the specimen with a hypotonic EDTA solution. The hypotonic solution lyses red blood cells, but leaves WBCs intact. WBCs are separated by centrifugation, forming a WBC "pellet" in the bottom of the centrifuge tube. The supernatant, containing hemoglobin, plasma proteins, and other soluble components from the lysed red cells or plasma is poured off leaving a relatively clean WBC pellet. The pellet is resuspended in the same hypotonic EDTA solution, and the tube is again centrifuged and decanted, in order to further wash away contaminating proteins and hemoglobin. The WBC pellet is further lysed by WBC lysis buffer which contain SDS. Further the sample is subjected to phenol chloroform method of DNA isolation get purified DNA.

Procedure

-Take 600ul of blood sample in a sterile microfuge tube and add 1 ml of TE buffer to that and mix well by tapping the tube.

-Centrifuge at 6000 rpm for 10 min.

-Discard the supernatant and add 1 ml of ice cold RBC lysis solution . Homogenize the suspension by inverting the tube several times

- Centrifuge at 6000 rpm for 10 min at 4oC

-Discard the supernatant and to the pellet add 800ul of WBC lysis solution

-Incubate at 60oC for 1 hour in a water bath, after incubation allow the sample to cool to room temperature

-Add 1ml of phenol-chloroform-isoamyl alcohol and mix well

-Centrifuge at 10000 rpm for 10 minutes

-After centrifugation three layers of solution could be observed in the eppendorf tube. Handle the tube carefully

-Using a 200ul pipette tip in the lower volume set carefully remove the upper aqueous phase to a fresh tube

-Add double the volume of ice-cold isopropanol to the aqueous phase and mix well

-Incubate at cold conditions for 1-2 hours for effective precipitation of DNA

-The precipitated DNA is then washed with 70% ethanol for 2-3 times and followed by air drying.

-Air dried DNA is dissolved in 50ul of 1X TE and stored for future use

CHAPTER SEVENTEEN

Isolation of plasmid DNA

AIM

To isolate the plasmid DNA from bacteria BY ALKALINE LYSIS METHOD

INTRODUCTION

DNA of prokaryotic cells is relatively simple in comparison to that of eukaryotic cells. In addition to chromosomal DNA, a bacterium may also carry an additional piece of DNA called a plasmid. Bacterial plasmids are double stranded closed circular DNA molecules that range in size from 1 kb to more than 200kb. Plasmids are useful to bacterial cells since they carry genes for antibody resistance, RM system etc that allow bacteria to survive in non-ideal conditions.

Plasmids constructed in the laboratory are used as cloning vehicles. These synthetic plasmids contain only essential features such as origin of replication, antibiotic resistance, multiple cloning sites etc.

ALKALINE LYSIS, IN COMBINATION WITH THE DETERGENT SDS, has been used for more than 20 years to isolate plasmid DNA from E. coli (Birnboim and Doly 1979). This experiment describes how to extract plasmid from bacteria – which involves growth of bacterial culture, harvesting and lysis of bacteria and isolation of plasmid DNA from the lysate using alkaline lysis method. The DNA is analyzed on agarose gel.

This method exploits the relatively small size and covalently closed circular nature of plasmid DNA. The bacterial cell pellet obtained after growing and harvesting is treated with different solutions.

PRINCIPLE

Exposure of bacterial suspensions to the strongly anionic detergent at high pH opens the cell wall, denatures chromosomal DNA and proteins, and releases plasmid DNA into the supernatant. Although the alkaline solution completely disrupts base pairing, the strands of closed circular plasmid DNA are unable to separate from each other because they are topologically intertwined. As long as the intensity and duration of exposure to OH- is not too great, the two strands of plasmid DNA fall once again into register when the pH is returned to neutral. During lysis, bacterial proteins, broken cell walls, and denatured chromosomal DNA become enmeshed in large complexes that are coated with dodecyl sulfate. These complexes are efficiently precipitated from solution when sodium ions are replaced by potassium ions (salting out). After the denatured material has been removed by centrifugation, native plasmid

DNA can be recovered from the supernatant. Strands of covalently closed circular (CCC) plasmid DNA unable to separate because of intertwining, renatures immediately and completely when conditions return to normal. The genomic DNA forms an aggregate with SDS and proteins.

MATERIALS REQUIRED

LB medium, Bacterial strain (Containing plasmid) Solution I, II and III, Ampicillin, Isopropanol or absolute ethanol, 1X TE, 70% Ethanol, Tabletop centrifuge, Dry bath, Microwave/ heater, 370C Shaker, incubator

PROCEDURE

Note: Streaking & inoculation should be done aseptically.

DAY 1: Streak the given bacterial culture on LB Agar containing Ampicillin (100ug/ml). Incubate at 370C. (Inverted) overnight.

DAY2: Inoculate a single colony into 5ml of LB medium containing 100ug/ml Ampicillin. Incubate at 370C with shaking for 8-16 hrs.

DAY3: Refer to the flowchart and follow the steps carefully. (For harvesting and alkali lysis)

1. Transfer 1.5ml overnight grown culture into eppendorf tube and centrifuge for 5 minutes at 6000 rpm.
2. Drain the supernatant and gently tap the tube inverted on a paper towel to remove the excess medium.
3. Add 100ul of solution I to the pellet and mix the contents by finger flicking the tube. No visible clumps of bacteria should remain. Incubate the tube at 40C for 5 minutes.

(Glucose in this solution provides an isosmotic condition to prevent physical shock. The resuspended solution's pH is raised to basic level with Tris to help denature DNA. EDTA stabilizes the cell membrane by binding the divalent cations. RNase will destroy RNA from the cell contents when the membrane is lysed).

4. Add 200ul of solution II and gently mix the contents by inverting the tube

4-5 times. The cell suspension should look clear at this stage
(The sodium dodecyl sulfate (SDS) is an ionic detergent, which dissolves the phospholipids and protein components of the cell membrane. Sodium hydroxide (NaOH) in the solution denatures the Plasmid and the chromosomal DNA into single strands).

5. Add 150ul of solution III and mix the contents by inverting the tube 4-5 times.

(Sodium acetate from this solution forms an insoluble precipitate of SDS / lipid / protein complex and neutralizes the sodium hydroxide from the previous step. At this neutral pH, the DNA renature. The chromosomal DNA is trapped in the SDS / lipid / protein precipitate. The Plasmid DNA renatures into its double stranded form and escapes being trapped in the precipitate and remains in the supernatant).

6. Centrifuge the tube containing lysate at 10,000 rpm for 15 minutes. (White precipitate is seen on the wall of the tube).

7. Gently transfer the supernatant into a fresh tube without disturbing the pellet. (The pellet is gooey and suddenly can slip into the tube). Add double volume of absolute ethanol slowly from the wall of the tube and incubate the tube at 40C for 30minutes.

8. Centrifuge at 10,000rpm for 15 minutes.

9. Carefully drain off the supernatant and mark the pellet.

10. When the pellet turns transparent, add 50ul of 1X TE to the pellet and resuspend by finger flicking. (This is your Plasmid DNA preparation, should contain 4-5ug of DNA).

11.Prepare an agarose gel of 1%.

12.Load 10-15ul of your DNA sample after addition of gel loading dye and run the gel at 100V for 30-40 minutes. Visualize with UV doc system and note the observation

OBSERVATION

A good preparation results in only super coiled DNA. Other forms – nicked and linear may be seen depending on the preparation. Sometimes chromosomal DNA may be seen in the preparation

CHAPTER EIGHTEEN

Determination of purity and concentration of genomic DNA samples

Aim

To determine the purity and concentration of genomic DNA isolated using Phenol chloroform method

Theory

The most common technique to determine DNA yield and purity is measurement of absorbance. Although it could be argued that fluorescence measurement is easier, absorbance measurement is simple, and requires commonly available laboratory equipment. All that is needed for the absorbance method is a spectrophotometer equipped with a UV lamp, UV-transparent cuvettes (depending on the instrument) and a solution of purified DNA. Absorbance readings are performed at 260nm (A260) where DNA absorbs light most strongly, and the number generated allows one to estimate the concentration of the solution. To ensure the numbers are useful, the A260 reading should be within the instrument's linear range (generally 0.1–1.0).

DNA concentration is estimated by measuring the absorbance at 260nm, adjusting the A260 measurement for turbidity (measured by absorbance at 320nm), multiplying by the dilution factor, and using the relationship that an A260 of 1.0 = 50µg/ml pure dsDNA.

Concentration (µg/ml) = (A260 reading – A320 reading) × dilution factor × 50µg/ml

To evaluate DNA purity, measure absorbance from 230nm to 320nm to detect other possible contaminants. The most common purity calculation is the ratio of the absorbance at 260nm divided by the reading at 280nm. Good-quality DNA will have an A260/A280 ratio of 1.7–2.0. A reading of 1.6 does not render the DNA unsuitable for any application, but lower ratios indicate more contaminants are present. The ratio can be calculated after correcting for turbidity (absorbance at 320nm).

DNA purity (A260/A280) = (A260 reading – A320 reading) ÷ (A280 reading – A320 reading)

Strong absorbance around 230nm can indicate that organic compounds or chaotropic salts are present in the purified DNA. A ratio of 260nm to 230nm can help evaluate the level of salt carryover in the purified DNA. The lower the ratio, the greater the amount of thiocyanate salt is present, for example. As a guideline, the A260/A230 is best if greater than 1.5. A reading at 320nm will indicate if there is turbidity in the solution, another indication of possible contamination. Therefore, taking a spectrum of readings from 230nm to 320nm is most informative.

Calculation

Concentration of DNA

Concentration (µg/ml) = (A260 reading – A320 reading) × dilution factor × 50µg/ml

Purity of DNA

DNA purity (A260/A280) = (A260 reading – A320 reading) ÷ (A280 reading – A320 reading)

A260/A230 =

CHAPTER NINETEEN

Lambda DNA Restriction Digestion

AIM

Restriction Endonuclease digestion of λ (Lambda) DNA by EcoRI.

Introduction

The primary tools used by the molecular biologists in manipulating DNA are restriction enzymes and other DNA/RNA modifying enzymes. Over the years, the number and uses of these enzymes have increased as new molecules have been discovered. Restriction endonucleases are bacterial enzymes that cleave double-stranded DNA. They are present in bacteria presumably to destroy DNA from foreign sources. By cleaving the foreign DNA at specific sites. The host bacterial DNA is protected from cleavage because specific recognition sites are modified, usually by methylation form methylase at one of the bases in the site, making the site no longer a substrate for RE cleavage. Host bacteria used to propagate cloned DNA in the laboratory are usually mutant in the host restriction genes, thus their intracellular enzyme activities will not destroy the foreign recombinant sequences. The Endonuclease with its accompanying Methylase is called a Restriction modification (R-M) system. At least four different kinds of R-M systems exist characterized on the basis of the subunit composition, cofactor requirements and type of DNA cleavage. Most characterized enzymes belong to type II class, together with type IIS class. They comprise the commercially available restriction enzymes used for DNA analysis and manipulation. Type I and Type III enzymes are relatively uncommon and a few additional enzymes fit none of the classes. Among more than 3000 different enzymes isolated from bacterial strains many share common specificities. Restriction enzymes that recognize identical sequences have been called as isoschizomers

Principle

All restriction enzymes cleave their DNA substrate to form 5'-phosphate and 3' hydroxyl termini on each strand. The breaks can be staggered, generating either 5' phosphate extension on each strand or 3'-hydroxyl extension on each strand, or they can be blunt ends. Type II restriction enzymes have been characterized primarily with respect to their recognition sequences and cleavage specifically rather than their protein properties. The symmetrical recognition sequence of restriction enzymes is termed as palindromes and is of four to eight base pairs. Most. But not all, recognition sequences contain dyad axis symmetry and in most case all the bases within the site are uniquely specified. Those with degenerate or relaxed specificities can recognize multiple bases at some positions. The enzyme EcoR1 recognizes the following recognition sequence and it gives cohesive (Sticky) end or the break is staggered.

DEFINITION OF UNIT

One unit enzyme is defined as the amount of enzyme required to completely digest one microgram of lambda DNA in a reaction volume of 50µl in 1 hour under optimal conditions of salt, pH and temperature. All digestions are performed at 37oC, unless noted otherwise.

Factors affecting optimum activity

1. **Temperature:** The optimal digestion of DNA varies over a wide temperature range for different restriction enzymes.

2. **Buffer Systems:** Tris-Cl is the most commonly used buffering agent in incubation mixtures. The buffer system is markedly temperature dependent. The change in pH/10 deg amounts to approximately 0.3.

3. **Ionic Conditions:** Mg2+ ions are an absolute requirement for all restriction endonucleases, whereas the addition of other salt components depends on different nucleases. If different ionic conditions are required for, site-specific cleavage with two or more restriction endonucleases the DNA is to be digested first with the enzyme with an optimum activity at low

ionic strength.

4. **Methylation of DNA**: Because restriction endonucleases are a part of prokaryotic restriction/modification system, digestion of DNA can be strongly affected by Methylation of specific adenine or cytidine residues within the recognition sequence of the site-specific restriction enzyme of interest.

PRINCIPLE

EcoR1 has 5 recognition sites on Bacteriophage λ DNA. λ DNA is the linear double stranded DNA having 48,502 base pairs. In this experiment, the substrate for EcoR1 is DNA. The position of 5 recognition sites on λ DNA are: 21226, 26104, 31747, 39168 and 44972. Upon complete digestion of the substrate under optimal conditions 6 fragments are released whose molecular weights are 21,226 bp, 7421 bp, 5804 bp, 5643 bp, 4878 bp and 3530 bp. Therefore, fragment sizes of the digested sample can be assessed by electrophoresing along with the standard molecular weight marker

MATERIALS REQUIRED

Substrate DNA such as Bacteriophage λ(Lambda) DNA or plasmid DNA, Restriction Enzymes, Assay buffers, Nuclease buffers, Nuclease free water, 50X TAE buffer, Agarose, Ethidium bromide, Gel loading Dye, Dry bath, Microfuge, Gel tank, combs, cords and power supply, Microwave/heater

PROCEDURE

1. Check the name of the given enzyme and DNA, note the concentrations respectively. Find out the suitable buffer for the enzyme.
2. Thaw the buffer vials stored at -20°C
3. Perform the digestion Lambda DNA with EcoR1 / Hind III endonucleases in a 1.5 mL microcentrifuge tube. Make the additions as indicated below.

Description	Test Reaction Mixture	Control Reaction Mixture
Lambda DNA	5 µL	5 µL
EcoR1/Hind III Activity Assay Buffer (10X)	2.5 µL	-
Distilled Water	16.5 µL	20 µL
EcoR1/ Hind III	1 µL	-

Mix the contents gently by finger flicking after each addition

Note:

§ Enzyme is thermolabile.

§ Use fresh tip for each addition

4. Incubate at 37°C (or at optimal temperature of the enzyme activity) for 1 hour.

5. Meanwhile prepare 1.0% agarose gel.

6. Stop the reaction by adding 3µl gel loading dye, mix the contents.

7. Load the samples into the will carefully and run the gel for about 1 hour (till the dye reaches the end of the gel)

8. Visualize gel under UV light and note down the observations.

CHAPTER TWENTY

Bacterial Transformation

Aim

To carry out Transformation of Competent cells by Heat shock method.

Introduction

Transformation results from the uptake of purified DNA by bacterial cells and is the most frequently used procedure for introducing recombinant DNA molecules into bacteria. It is now widely used to transfer small plasmids from one bacterial strain to another. DNA is extracted from donor cell and used to treat the recipient cells that have been rendered more susceptible to DNA uptake. These competent cells allow DNA to enter through pores or channels in the cell membrane and in the case of plasmids, permit subsequent plasmid replication.

Principle

Some species of bacteria naturally take up DNA at a certain stage of growth called competence. Some species however are not naturally competent at any stage of growth. Competence can be artificially induced in these cells by treating them with CaCl2 prior to adding DNA. The Ca 2+ destabilizes the cell membrane and a Ca –Phosphate - DNA complex is formed which adheres to the cell surface and is resistant to DNases. The DNA is taken up during a heat shock step when the cells are exposed briefly to a temperature of 42^0 C. immediately chilling on ice ensures closure of pores. Selection for cells containing transformed DNA is greatly enhanced by the selection marker carried by the DNA. pUC series and pBR 322 have ampicillin resistance factor which enables only the transformed cells to grow on LB Ampicillin plates.

The pUC plasmids also have the gene for β- galactosidase (lac Z) from *E. coli.* The lac Z gene has a series of unique restriction sites engineered into it such that the plasmid can be cut within the lac Z gene. If these plasmids are transformed into a lac Z strain of E-coli. They will make them Lac+. Although neither the host nor the plasmid encoded fragments are themselves active, they can associate to form an enzymatically active protein. This type of complementation is known as alpha complementation.

Lac+ bacteria that result from alpha complementation can be recognized as they form blue colonies in presence of X-gal (as β-galactosidase cleaves this chromogenic substrate) and IPTG (that acts as an inducer for the expression of the enzyme).

Any plasmid which has a DNA fragment cloned into it (lac Z genes site) will not have a functional lac Z gene and thus will produce white colonies which are unable to cleave X-gal

Procedure

The experiment should be done strictly under aseptic conditions.

PREPARATION OF COMPETENT CELLS:

This procedure allows the preparation of cells that can be used immediately

Revival of host strain:

1. Streak DH 5α strain provided as lyophilized vial onto a fresh LB plate to get a single colony. Incubate the plate overnight at 37^{0}C.

2. Pick a single colony the following day and incubate in the evening into 5ml LB medium. Incubate the tube O/N at 37^{0}C for about 16 to 18 hrs.

3. On the third day, begin the preparation of competent cells as outlined.

A. Transfer the 5ml O/N saturated culture into 100ml LB medium and incubate at 37^{0}C Grow until the OD (A600) reaches 0.23-0.26 (it takes around 2-3 hrs to reach the required OD).

B. Once the OD is reached quickly chill the culture flask on ice and leave it on ice in refrigerator for 10-20 mins (from this point all work done at 4^{0}C)

C. Transfer 1.5ml culture aseptically into sterile microfuge tube and spin down at 6000 rpm for 8 min (if you have a refrigerated centrifuge spin at 4^{0}C)

D. Discard the supernatant and to the cell pellet add 1ml of 0.1 M $CaCl_2$ suspend the cell pellet gently in CaCl2 and this should be done by keeping the tubes in ice bucket. Keep on ice for 30 mins. Centrifuge at 6000 rpm for

8 mins.

E. Discard the supernatant and resuspend the pellet gently in 0.2ml $CaCl_2$.

NOTE: $CaCl_2$ Solution: Make required quantity of 0.1M $CaCl_2$ from the stock solution provided to you. Use autoclaved water only. While resuspending keep your centrifuge tube on ice. O.1M $CaCl_2$ should be ice cold.

TRANSFORMATION PROCEDURE:

1. To the 100 µl of competent cells prepared add 5µl of the DNA (100ng) provided. Gently tap and keep the vial on ice for 20 minutes.

2. Prepare a water bath at 42^{0}C. Keep the vial in the water bath such that the competent cells are immersed for 2 minutes. The temp should be maintained accurately during this period.

3. Quickly remove the vial after heat shock and chill the vial on ice for 20 minutes.

4. Add 0.8ml of LB aseptically to the vial and incubate the culture for 1 hour at 37^{0}C to allow bacteria to recover and express the antibiotic resistance.

5. Preparation of LB Amp. Plates: when the agar is around 44^{0}C, add 100µg per ml of antibiotic, 40µl of X-Gal & IPTG each for every 20 ml of agar, mix well and pour into petri plates.

PLATING:

Transfer 10µl, 25µl, 50µl, and 100µl of step 4 to each plate. Add 100µl of LB broth on top of the inoculums, mix well and spread thoroughly using a pipette or spreader. A control plate with competent cells that receive no plasmid DNA should also be plated to rule out contamination of cells.

ANTIBIOTIC PREPARATION: Dissolve required quantity of the antibiotic in sterile water and store at 4^{0}C Make antibiotic fresh, just before use, ADD ONLY AFTER THE MEDIUM IS COOL ENOUGH

CHAPTER TWENTY-ONE

Blood group Typing

Aim

To determine the blood group of the given human blood sample

Materials & Apparatus Used

Monoclonal Antibodies (Anti-A, B and D)
Blood Lancet
Alcohol swabs
Tooth picks
Sterile cotton balls
Clean glass slide

Procedure

- Set the table with all the materials required including Monoclonal Antibody (Mab) kit
- Open an Alcohol swab, and rub it at the area from where the blood will be sampled (fingertip). (Discard the swab)
- Open the Lancet cover, put pressure at the tip of the finger from where blood will be sampled (maintain it). Prick the fingertip with the opened Lancet.(Discard the Lancet)
- As blood starts oozing out, make 3 drops fall into a clean glass slide forming 3 blood spots.
- Place a cotton ball at the site where it was pricked. Using the thumb, put pressure on the area to stop blood flow.
- Take the Anti-A (blue) bottle, resuspend the content and use the dropper to place a drop of the Mab in the 1st spot.
- Take the Anti-B (yellow) bottle, resuspend the content and use the dropper to place a drop of the Mab in the 2nd spot.
- Take the Anti-D (colorless) bottle, resuspend the content and use the dropper to place a drop of the Mab in the 3rd spot.

- Take a tooth pick and mix the content in each well. Discard the tooth pick after using in one well (take a new one for the next well).
- After mixing, wait for a while to observe for the agglutination in the spots.

CHAPTER TWENTY-TWO

Blood smear/film preperation

Aim

To prepare blood film and identify blood cells

Apparatus Used

Blood Sample, Slides, Alcohol 70%, Blood Lancet, Spirit, Cotton, Leishman stain

Procedure

BLOOD SMEAR PREPARATION

The aim of preparing smears is to spread out the cells for identification with a minimum of damage. This requires the use of good quality, oil-free slides with an even edge and surface

• Rest a frosted glass slide on firm support and place a small drop of blood just in from one end of the slide.

• Place the spreader slide at approximately 30 -40° in front of the drop and move the spreader back until it just touches the drop. The drop will immediately run along the edge of the spreader slide.

• With the same angle of the spreader slide, move it smoothly along until the smear is approximately 3 cm in length.

• Thick viscous blood may be spread rapidly with the spreader slide at a lower angle.

• Thin anaemic blood should be spread slowly with the spreader held at a greater angle (up to 70 - 80°).

• The finished smear should have a nicely rounded tail. This is achieved by using the correct amount of blood and spreading technique. The red cells should lie side by side with minimal distortion and the white cells should be well spread.

• Allow the smear to dry in air at room temperature. Waving the smear in the air or holding over a gas flame or hair dryer can be used to hasten the process. Direct drying of the smear with blotting paper or filter paper is not recommended because it damages the cells.

- Fix the smears by dipping them in absolute methanol (optional)

PRECAUTIONS TO BE TAKEN DURING PREPARATION:

- Angle should be maintained at 45°.
- Blood drop should be of proper size.
- Spreader's edges should be smooth and it should be smaller than the slide on which smear is being made.
- Pressure applied should be proper.
- Drop should be pulled with spreader not pushed with it.
- Preparation should be in one single stroke.

STAINING OF BLOOD FILM

- Cover the well dried, thin blood smear with undiluted Leishman Stain solution by counting the drops (3-4) of Leishman stain.
- Let it stand for 2-3 minutes, the methanol present in the stain fixes the smear onto the glass slide.
- After 2-3 minutes, add twice the amount of distilled water or Phosphate buffer solution and mix the content by swirling or by blowing gently.
- Incubate the slides for at least 10 min at 37 °C. This will stain the blood cells (optional)
- Air dry the slides in a tilted position so that the water easily removes out of the slides.
- Observe the slides under oil immersion objective lens of the microscope.

PRECAUTIONS DURING STAINING:

- Time: Initial time 2 minutes, is important. After dilution increase of 1-2 minutes, does not alter staining.
- Never let the stain dry on the slide otherwise stain deposits will make it impossible to count leucocytes.
- Stain should be deposit free.
- For washing the smear – let the water stream replace the stain. Don not throws the stain first.

Observations

Various types of blood cells were observed

CHAPTER TWENTY-THREE

Separation of plasma and serum from blood

Aim

To effectively separate blood components

Materials & Apparatus Used

Serum (needs clot time)

A serum separator tube (SST, tiger top tube).

Let the blood sit for 30 minutes to one hour at room temperature to clot before spinning and separating.

A delay in centrifugation may have a detrimental effect on the sample quality and may result inaccurate results. Avoid hemolysis.

Separating plasma (time sensitive)

Tube with an anti-coagulant eg: Edta (lavender top) sodium heparin (green top), sodium citrate (blue top) are used for separating Plasma

You need to spin and separate within one hour of receiving the specimen (time sensitive)

Procedure

Separation of plasma

1) Blood will be collected into purple top EDTA tubes and centrifuged (2000 rpm) at 4 degrees centigrade for 20 minutes.

2) After centrifugation using clean pipette technique place 1.0ml of plasma into 1.5ml eppendorf tube labeled with tracking number and "plasma"

3) Freeze immediately at –80 degree freezer

Separation of Serum

1. A 10 ml tube of whole blood will be collected following standard procedures using a serum separator tube (SST, tiger top tube) from each patient.

2. Allow samples to clot for one hour at room temperature

3. Centrifuge for 10 minutes at approximately 1000g

4. Using clean pipette technique Aliquot 210ul of serum into labeled cryovials. 5. Immediately freeze vials of serum at –80-degree freezer

Aliquoting whole blood

Whole blood will be aliquoted into sterile tubes upon receipt by carefully inverting the blood tube so that it is gently mixed before pipetting appropriate amounts (protocol specific) of whole blood into appropriate storage tubes using clean pipette tips between each patient.

- Gently invert the tube of blood to mix contents
- Carefully open blood tube (universal precautions; gloves, eye protection)
- With clean pipette tip aliquot appropriate amount of whole blood into clean/labeled storage tubes.

Observations

Serum and Plasma is separated from blood

CHAPTER TWENTY-FOUR

Ouchterlony Double Diffusion

Aim

To study the reaction pattern of an antigen with a set of antibodies by Ouchterlony Double Diffusion method.

Materials & Apparatus Used

Kit Contents: This kit can be used to determine the relationship between the antigens and antibodies using Ouchterlony.

Glass wares: Measuring cylinder, Beaker

Reagents: Alcohol, Distilled Water

Other requirements: Incubator (37oC), Microwave or Bunsen burner, Vortex mixer, Spatula, Micropipettes, Tips, Moist chamber (box with wet cotton)

Procedure

- Prepare 10 ml of 1% agarose (as given in important instructions).
- Cool the solution to 55-60°C and pour 5 ml/plate on to grease free glass plates placed on a horizontal surface. Allow the gel to set for 30 minutes.
- Place the glass plate on the template provided.
- Punch wells with the help of the gel puncher corresponding to the markings on the template. Use gentle suction to avoid forming of rugged wells.
- Add 10 µl each of the antiserum and the corresponding antigens to the wells.
- Keep the glass plate in a moist chamber overnight at 37°C.
- After incubation, observe for opaque precipitin lines between the antigen and antiserum wells.

Observations

Observation for presence of precipitin lines between antigen and antisera wells.

CHAPTER TWENTY-FIVE

Dot ELISA

Aim

To learn the technique of Dot ELISA for the detection of an antigen.

Materials & Apparatus Used

Kit Contents: This kit can be used to detect the presence of a test antigen by immobilized antibody bound to the membrane followed by binding of the antigen to the labeled secondary antibody and its detection by using appropriate substrate.

Glass wares: Test tubes

Reagents: Distilled Water

Other requirements: Micropipette, Tips

Procedure

- Take 2 ml of 1X Assay Buffer in a test tube and add 2 μl of the test serum sample. Mix thoroughly by pipetting. Insert a Dot-ELISA strip into the tube.
- Incubate the tube at room temperature for 20 minutes. Discard the solution.
- Wash the strip two times by dipping it in 2 ml of 1X Assay Buffer for about 5 minutes each. Replace the buffer each time.
- Take 2 ml of 1X Assay Buffer in a fresh test tube, add 2 μl of HRP conjugated antibody to it. Mix thoroughly by pipetting. Dip the ELISA strip into it and allow the reaction to take place for 20 minutes.
- Wash the strip as in step # 3 for two times.
- In a collection tube (provided in the kit) take 1.3 ml of TMB/H2O2 and dip the ELISA strip into this substrate solution.
- Observe the strip after 5 - 10 minutes for the appearance of a blue spot.
- Rinse the strip with distilled water

Observations

Look for the appearance of the blue dot (depend on the kit used)

CHAPTER TWENTY-SIX

Preparation of hemin crystals from human blood

Aim

To prepare hemin crystals from human blood sample

Principle & Significance

Hemin (haemin; ferric chloride heme) is an iron-containing porphyrin with chlorine that can be formed from a haem group, such as haem b found in the hemoglobin of human blood. Hemin can be produced from hemoglobin by the so called Teichmann test, when hemoglobin is heated with glacial acetic acid (saturated with saline). This can be used to detect blood traces.

Materials required

Human blood
Lancet
Cotton
Alcohol
Glass slides
Sodium chloride
Glacial acetic acid
Spirit lamp
Microscope

Protocol

- A drop of blood is taken on a glass slide and spread it up using a spreader slide.
- Dry the blood in air
- Crush the dried blood to a fine powder with the help of the fused end of a glass rod or with a needle.

- One crystal of common salt (NaCI) is added to it, which is also crushed to powder.
- The two are thoroughly mixed and two drops of glacial acetic acid added to it.
- The mixture is covered with a cover slip and the slide heated over the flame of a spirit lamp.
- The reaction is complete with the beginning of boiling of the mixture and the slide is quickly removed from the flame.
- The preparation is allowed to cool and examine under a microscope, initially under low magnification and then under high magnification

Results and Conclusions

Rhomboidal crystals arranged on star shaped clusters with round edges where observed

CHAPTER TWENTY-SEVEN

Qualitative tests to identify functional groups of carbohydrates in given solutions

Aim

This experiment aims to introduce you with the identification of unknown carbohydrates

Principle & Significance

A carbohydrate is an organic compound with the general formula Cm(H2O)n, that is, consists only of carbon, hydrogen and oxygen, with the last two in the 2:1 atom ratio. The carbohydrates (saccharides) are divided into four chemical groups: monosaccharides, disaccharides, oligosaccharides and polysaccharides. Carbohydrates on reaction with certain solutions which can give insights into their identity and knowledge about their functional groups thereby helping in the identification of sugars.

Materials required

Sugar Solutions (Glucose, Fructose, Sucrose and Galactose)

Test Reagents (Molish, Benedicts, Barfoed, Seliwanoff and Fehling)

Test tube

Pipettes

Water bath

Molisch's Test

Principle

Molisch's Test is a sensitive chemical test for all carbohydrates, and some compounds containing carbohydrates in a combined form, based on the dehydration of the carbohydrate by sulfuric acid to produce an aldehyde (either furfural or a derivative), which then condenses with the phenolic structure resulting in a red or purple-colored compound.

Protocol

- Place 2 mL of a known carbohydrate solution in a test tube, add 1 drop of Molisch's reagent (10% α-naphthol in ethanol).
- Pour 1-2 mL of conc. H2SO4 down the side of the test tube, so that it forms a layer at the bottom of the tube.
- Observe the color at the interface between two layers and compare your result with a control test.

Result

Reddish ring is observed at junction between two layers. Presence of carbohydrates is confirmed.

Fehling's Test

Principle

Fehling's Solution (deep blue colored) is used to determine the presence of reducing sugars and aldehydes.

Protocol

- To 1 mL of Fehling's solution A (aqueous solution of CuSO4) add 1 mL of Fehling solution B (solution of potassium tartrate).
- Add 2 mL of the sugar solution, mix well and boil.
- Observe the red precipitate of cuprous oxide that forms at the end of the reaction.

Result

Red precipitate was observed in glucose, fructose and galactose. Sucrose found to be negative in reaction.

Barfoed's Test

Principle

Barfoed's reagent, cupric acetate in acetic acid, is slightly acidic and is balanced so that is can only be reduced by monosaccharides but not less powerful reducing sugars. Disaccharides may also react with this reagent, but the reaction is much slower when compared to monosaccharides..

Protocol

- To 1-2 mL of Barfoed's reagent, add an equal volume of sugar solution.
- Boil for 5 min. in a water bath and allow to stand.
- Observe a brick-red cuprous oxide precipitate if reduction has taken place

Result

Brick red precipitate was observed in glucose, fructose and galactose. Sucrose found to be negative in reaction.

Seliwanoff's Test

Principle

Seliwanoff's Test distinguishes between aldose and ketose sugars. Ketoses are distinguished from aldoses via their ketone/aldehyde functionality. If the sugar contains a ketone group, it is a ketose and if it contains an aldehyde group, it is an aldose. This test is based on the fact that, when heated, ketoses are more rapidly dehydrated than aldoses.

Protocol

- Heat 1 mL of sugar solution with 3 mL Seliwanoff's reagent (0.5 g resorcinol per liter 10% HCl) in boiling water.
- In less than 30 seconds, a red color must appear for ketoses

Result

Fructose only given a positive reaction with a cherry red color.

Benedict's test

Principle

Free aldehyde or ketone group of sugars have the ability to reduce solutions of metallic ions like copper giving rise to green to red colored precipitate.

Protocol

- Take 5 mL of Benedict's reagent in a test tube
- Add 8 drops of sugar solution to it
- Boil over a flame or boiling water bath for 2 min
- Observe the color change in the solution.

Result

Red color precipitate was observed in all tubes except sucrose

CHAPTER TWENTY-EIGHT

Study of activity of salivary amylase under optimum conditions

Aim

To study the activity of salivary amylase under optimal conditions

Principle & Significance

Salivary amylase is a powerful enzyme. It can react with starch to give dextrin, di and monosaccharides. The reaction of starch with salivary amylase can be visualized by adding iodine to the reaction mixture. Normally the reaction of starch with iodine gives a deep blue color. The breakdown of starch by salivary amylase can produce characteristic changes in the color of the reaction mixture. Dextrin can give dark brown to red color to the reaction mixture while if mono or di saccharides are present can change the color of the mixture to dark brown to yellowish in color. This color change can be used to study the activity of salivary amylase.

Materials required

Saliva
Starch
Iodine
Distilled water
Water bath
Test tubes

Protocol

- Collect 2 mL of saliva and dilute it to 100 mL using distilled water. Stir the solution to make sure the enzyme is spread evenly.

- Add 4 drops of iodine in one test tube
- In another test tube mix 1mL of diluted saliva, 4 mL starch and 1 mL distilled water. Put this mixture in water bath at 37oC for 3 min. This is the reaction mixture
- Add 5 drops of reaction mixture to 4 drops of iodine in the initial test tube. Mix it well.
- Observe the color change in interval of 1min up to 7 minutes.

Results and Conclusions

Color change from deep blue to dark brown was observed in the 7 minute

CHAPTER TWENTY-NINE

Writing Review of Literature

Aim

To understand and learn how to write a review of literature

Introduction

What Is a Literature Review?

A literature review is a survey of scholarly articles, books, or other sources that pertain to a specific topic, area of research, or theory. The literature review offers brief descriptions, summaries, and critical evaluations of each work, and does so in the form of a well organized essay. Scholars often write literature reviews to provide an overview of the most significant recent literature published on a topic. They also use literature reviews to trace the evolution of certain debates or intellectual problems within a field. Even if a literature review is not a formal part of a research project, students should conduct an informal one so that they know what kind of scholarly work has been done previously on the topic that they have selected.

How Is a Literature Review Different from a Research Paper?

An academic research paper attempts to develop a new argument, and typically has a literature review as one of its parts. In a research paper, the author uses the literature review to show how his or her new insights build upon and depart from existing scholarship. A literature review by itself does not try to make a new argument based on original research, but rather summarizes, synthesizes, and critiques the arguments and ideas of others, and points to gaps in the current literature.

Picking a Topic First,

the writer needs to pick a topic that she finds compelling and that is relevant to the course. Second, the topic should be relatively narrow so that it does not overwhelm the writer. For example, the literature on the causes of the U.S. Civil War is much too vast for a short review essay. A review of recent scholarship published on the economic impact of secession on the Confederacy is probably narrow enough for a relatively short essay. In most cases, students will need to clear a topic with the instructor before proceeding to make sure that it is a relevant topic of the proper scope.

Finding Relevant Literature

With the advent of electronic databases like Google scholar, JSTOR, Academic Search Complete, Lexis/Nexis, and Project Muse, it has become relatively easy to find relevant and trustworthy sources for a literature review essay. When searching these databases, the writer needs to use keywords or phrases that are as closely associated with the topic as possible. Searching with one or two phrases surrounded by quotation marks (for example, "Civil War" in tandem with "economic impact") will help to hone in on the most relevant results, as only articles that contain those two specific phrases will be found.

Evaluating the Literature

After students have found a number of articles or books related to a topic, they will evaluate them to determine which ones seem to make the most important contributions to the scholarship on the topic. In addition, evaluating articles with these questions will be helpful in figuring out how to organize the material later when composing the essay.

Organizing a Literature Review

A successful literature review should have three parts that break down in the following way:

A. INTRODUCTION

Defines and identifies the topic and establishes the reason for the literature review.

B. BODY OF THE REVIEW

Emphasizes the main findings or arguments of the articles in the student's own words. Analyse the articles to find common and contradictory findings and critically examine them.

C. CONCLUSION

Summarizes the major themes that emerged in the review and identifies areas of controversy

in the literature. Pinpoints strengths and weaknesses among the articles (innovative methods used, gaps in

research, problems with theoretical frameworks, etc.). Concludes by formulating questions that need further research within the topic, and provides some insight into the relationship between that topic and the larger field of study or discipline.

Exercise

Read the following three articles and answer the questions

Article #1

The loss of social relationships and emotional attachments have also evolved as a vital social impacts due to this COVID-19 pandemic. The lockdown and the social distancing factors have secluded individuals. This has also led to the psychological issues among the human beings. The lack of traveling arrangements has also been observed as the poor migrant workers had to walk thousands of kilometers. Introduction of internet connected devices in the medical field during this COVID-19 pandemic has helped to disseminate proper information [2]. Various clinical considerations for patients with diabetes during the COVID- 19 epidemic have also been discussed [3].

The persons with the diseases and the earlier illness are also getting impacted under this lockdown and pandemic terms due to lack of proper interaction with the physicians. The cases of diabetes, hypertensions, etc. are some of the few who have been affected during this time. The bad impacts of this lockdown has also been seen in terms of the increased body weight due to the unbalanced life style, over eating, no outdoor activities, over sleep, etc. which have further deteriorated the health conditions. The daily exercise and the walking habits of the individuals have also got affected. As reported around 19% have gained weight and around 42% of the persons are not performing their routine exercises [1]. In related researches, some more latest and digital technologies have also been employed for confronting this pandemicsoon in this tougher time of COVID-19. While research is needed to arrive at a proper vaccine, more research is needed to address the related sectors affected badly by the pandemic.

Article #2

As part of the response to coronavirus disease 2019 (COVID-19), schools in Hong Kong did not resume after the Lunar New Year holiday at the end of January 2020. Classes were instead scheduled online. Following a period without any local infections, secondary schools reopened in late May and primary schools reopened in the subsequent weeks. There were no cases in school-aged children until early July when local transmission resurged [2]. Schools were closed again on 13 July, 1 week before the scheduled summer break. By 18 July, there were 20 cases aged 5–17 years. Fifteen were linked to case clusters within their own household or neighbourhood or had unknown source of infection. The remaining cases included a secondary school cluster and a cluster at a tutorial centre.

Assuming that students were potentially infectious from 4 days before illness onset through 7 days after onset [3], many cases attended school while infectious (Figure). School-wide testing was conducted for schools attended by seven of the 15 cases and for the two clusters, and close contacts were placed under medical surveillance. No other cases related to these 20 cases have been identified in this age group since, suggesting that multiple potential introductions of COVID-19 into schools did not lead to onward transmission. This may be because children, especially young ones, could be less efficient spreaders of COVID-19 [4,5], supplemented by the protective effect of school-based precautionary measures.

Article #3

COVID-19 poses mental health risks to a range of vulnerable groups including those with active infection and those at higher risk of exposure such as healthcare workers. Studies following the 2003 SARS epidemic identified that individuals who were infected experienced significantly higher stress levels than healthy controls and healthcare workers with SARS even more so compared to other patients (Chua et al., 2004). A study showed that a quarter of the individuals who recovered from SARS infections had PTSD, and almost one sixth had depressive disorders years after SARS (Mak et al., 2009). During SARS, quarantined healthcare workers experienced fear, fueled by caregiver fatigue and stigma (Maunder et al., 2003), and were at higher risk for Acute Stress Disorder (Bai et al., 2004).

The social realities that the pandemic imposes also create a risk to patients with preexisting mental health conditions. We learned early in the COVID-19 pandemic that individuals with underlying cardiopulmonary and other medical comorbidities are at risk for increased morbidity and mortality (Shi et al., 2020). In contrast, little is known about acute and chronic risks associated with psychiatric comorbidities in the context of social distancing and "shelter-in-place" with the additional impact on access to care (Mak et al., 2010). Information regarding the intersection of mental illness and the social context of COVID-19 is critical to healthcare interventions and policy development.

A range of mental health morbidity occurs also within individual physiologic responses to the COVID-19 virus. Initial studies from Wuhan showed that one fifth of the individuals who died from SARS-CoV-2 had encephalopathy (Chen et al., 2020), possibly mediated by cytokine release in response to infection (Troyer et al., 2020). There are published reports ofICU delirium with COVID-19 (Kotfis et al., 2020), introducing concern for long-term complications such as depression, anxiety, and PTSD (Marra et al., 2017). This highlights the importance of attention to the long-term mental health sequelae for the patients who survive the ICU.

The secondary effects of the pandemic introduce additional challenges. Financial ramifications of job loss and work schedule changes may negatively impact mental health. "Essential workers" have the stress of increased exposure. Children at risk for abuse have fewer safety nets for protection in the absence of school based services (Campbell, 2020).

Preliminary data demonstrate racial and ethnic health outcome disparities in the current pandemic (Khunti et al., 2020). Considering these disparities and how they relate to mental health outcomes will also be crucial. Assessing mental health consequences and their potential treatments may identify opportunities for improved access to psychiatric interventions in the post-pandemic future. As health care systems are rapidly adopting telehealth in an effort to provide care while minimizing risk of exposure to COVID-19 (Hollander and Carr, 2020), we have an opportunity to assess telehealth's benefits for managing the ongoing needs of psychiatric patient populations. Early findings show that the already existing gaps in access to care in rural America persist with limited broadband access and reimbursement issues in these areas (Lee et al., 2020). Third party reimbursement for telehealth is increasing with the need for social distancing while still providing necessary health care. Health care systems have the potential to expand access through use of technology.

The conversation on mental health has already begun. Columnists draw attention to the negative effects of social isolation, and news sources collect survey data on respondent's mental health status (Brooks, 2020). Researchers are reviewing the impact of quarantine on mental health (Brooks et al., 2020), discussing psychological interventions in China (Duan and Zhu, 2020), and assessing potential strategies to mitigate COVID-19-provoked anxiety (Zheng et al., 2020). Corporations are seeking online mental health counseling for their employees, and universities are offering these resources to communities. Despite these efforts, we acknowledge the need for continued research and better definition of mental health consequences of COVID-19.

The pandemic's effects are pervasive and far-reaching. It is becoming clear that the consequences of COVID-19 go beyond the infection, and they highlight the biopsychosocial framing of illness on a global scale, including the secondary effects of the infection on mental health. With this in mind, studying the mental health ramifications of the COVID-19 pandemic should challenge us to examine the artificial dichotomy between physical and mental health. Notably, previous experience demonstrates that psychiatric consequences of global events and appropriate care for these consequences are influenced by culture. The scale of the pandemic and its reach across most of the world may afford a better understanding of how culture interfaces with mental illness. We may improve our understanding of how mental and physical health relate to one another in ways not previously recognized or acknowledged.

We find ourselves in a uniquely challenging time for our global society. The infection is not only manifesting neuropsychiatric effects but is also altering our cultural behavior, forcing us into a new way of life. The pandemic affects every aspect of our lives in ways that we do not yet fully grasp. The onus falls on us to describe these footprints and learn from themWe have an unprecedented opportunity to document and evaluate novel interventions for improving mental health. It is crucial for mental health to be incorporated into assessment of patient outcomes as well as into review of public health consequences. Only by matching the pace of change can we aspire to address mental health issues for all.

Exercise

1.Write down the theme (what the article says about) of the article

Article #1:

Write the theme in 1-2 sentences

Article #2

Write the theme in 1-2 sentences

Article #3

Write the theme in 1-2 sentences

2.Write down three major points discussed in the articles?

Article #1

1...................................

2....................................

3.....................................

Article #2

1......................................

2......................................

3.......................................

Article #3

1.......................................

2.......................................

3.......................................

3. Do you oppose or have different opinion in any of the things discussed in these three
articles?

4. Write down the common things observed in all the three articles?

5. Summarise the three articles in 1-2 paragraphs

This excercises will help you to understand how to analyse research data present manuscripts and which in turn help you to summarise it into reviews. You can now take more articles and try to write it into a full review.

CHAPTER THIRTY

Selection of research problem

Aim

To learn how to formulate research questions

Introduction

A research problem is a statement about an area of concern, a condition to be improved, a difficulty to be eliminated, or a troubling question that exists in scholarly literature, in theory, or in practice that points to the need for meaningful understanding and deliberate investigation. In some social science disciplines, the research problem is typically posed in the form of a question. A research problem does not state how to do something, offer a vague or broad proposition, or present a value question.

The 5Ws (and 1 H) that should be asked

The Five Ws and one H, are questions whose answers are considered basic in information-gathering.

They include Who, What, When Where, and Why.

Who does your topic impact? Who cares about your topic?

What is influenced by or influences your topic?

When was or is your topic relevant?

Where is your topic relevant?

Why is your topic important?

How it can be done?

Basic Steps in Formulating a Research Problem

The process of formulating a research problem requires a series of steps

(i) Identify the Broad Study Area

This is a great idea to thinking about the subject area of your interest. You should identify the field in which you would like to work a long time after your academic study or graduation. It will help you tremendously to get an interesting research topic.

For example- if you do post-graduation in Microbiology with specialisation in Microbial pathogenesis, you must decide your research study area in Tuberculosis or HIV etc. You might choose problems related with Mycobacterium pathogenesis, HIV reverse transcriptase etc.

(ii) Dissect the Broad Study Area into Subareas

In this stage, you need to dissect and specify your research broad study area into some subareas. You would consult with your supervisor in this regard. Write down subareas

(iii) Mark-up your Interest

It is almost impossible to study all subareas. That's why you must identify your area of interest. You should select issues in which you are passionate about. Your interest must be the most important determinant of your research study. Once you selected your research study of interest, you should delete other subareas in which you do not feel interested. Keep in mind that if you lose your interest in your research study it won't bring any results eventually.

(iv) Study Research Questions

In this step in formulating a research problem, you would point out your research questions under the area of interest as you decided in the previous stage. If you select unemployment as your study area,your questions might be "how unemployment impacts on individual social status?" "How it affects social stability?" "How it creates frustration on individuals?" Define what research problem or question you are going to study? The more you study the research problem it will be just as relevant and fruitful to solve the problem indeed.

Exercise

Select or Derive or Formulate Research Problem after reading following article

Infection with Mycobacterium tuberculosis resistant to isoniazid (H) and rifampicin (R) also called as MDR-TB or RR TB,1-3 leads to treatment with less potent, more toxic and expensive second-line anti- TB drugs (SLD). Fluoroquinolones (FQ) are crucial and integral part of drug resistant tuberculosis (DR-TB) treatment regimens1,3,4. Wide and illogic use of FQ, either for tuberculosis (TB) or other infections of respiratory tract, is responsible for increasing FQ resistance in MDR-TB, and lead to a situation where treatment options are narrowed1,3. FQ resistance and poor treatment outcomes in MDR-TB have been reported in studies4,5. Unfortunately, India has high TB burden and also is a high MDR-TB burden country,6 and by inference harbours large extensively-drug resistant tuberculosis (XDR-TB) population. FQ resistance may thus be a more prevalent than actually reported and can threaten TB control programmes1. Studies from India have demonstrated the prevalence of FQ resistance in MDR-TB patients1,3,7,8,9 but none from North Coastal Andhra Pradesh. Hence we studied the proportion of FQ resistance among MDR-TB/RR-TB and also the proportion of their crossresistance among MDR-TB/RR-TB isolates. WHO estimated incidence of MDR-TB/RR-TB in 2018 in India was 1,30,000.6 The first National Anti-Tuberculosis Drug Resistance Survey (NDRS) from India released on World TB Day, i.e., 24th March 2018 states incidence of MDR-TB is 6.19% (CI 5.54–6.90%) among all TB patients2,5.These figures are higher than that observed in the present study ie. MDR-TB/RR TB is 4.1% among all TB patients. Among MDR TB patients 89.1% of rifampicin monoresistant patients were detected by GeneXpert/ CBNAAT and LPA methods. All rifampicin monoresistance were considered as MDR-TB and initiated on MDR-TB treatment under RNTCP as rifampicin monoresistance is considered as surrogate marker for MDR-TB2,7. One of the key findings of the NDRS report is that almost all RR-TB patients are resistant to isoniazid with or without other first or second line drugs2.

FQ especially Mfx, are integral part of standard regimen (shorter MDR-TB regimen and conventional MDR-TB regimen) for initiating treatment of MDR-TB/RR-TB at district DR-TB centre based on CBNAAT or FL-LPA2. FQ have the potential to become first line therapy for TB7. Latest Global tuberculosis report (2019), any FQ resistance among MDR-TB patients was 21 % globally6. In National Anti-Tuberculosis Drug Resistance Survey, additional resistance to FQ, among MDR-TB patients was shown to be 21.82 %2,5. Association of FQ resistance among individuals with resistance to firstline TB drugs is evidence of acquired FQ resistance while on treatment for TB3. In the current study, additional resistance to FQ, among MDR-TB patients was seen in 14.2% patients and was lower. It may be due to early diagnosis of MDR/RR TB and satisfactory treatment due to availability of quality assured drug susceptibility testing services in the state and the implementation of programmatic management of DR-TB under RNTCP 7–8 years back itself. Studies from other reference laboratories in India reported additional resistance to FQ among MDR-TB as 16.1% 3, 17.1% 3, 31% 8 & 33% 7 from isolates from Tamil Nadu, Kerala, Delhi and Karnataka respectively. The variations may be due to differences in study population and evolving DR-TB algorithms with time. The present study was performed after implementation of Universal DST. It may limit benefit of short course regime recommended by WHO for MDR-TB patients as resistance to FQ excludes the use of regime9. In a study from Uttar Pradesh, FQ resistance (with or without injectable SLD resistance) detected by second line LPA was high (58.4%) and stated those patients were not entitled for a shorter regimen9. Knowledge regarding individual's drug resistance pattern before would help in instituting appropriate treatment regimen avoiding transmission of extensively DR-TB (XDR-TB) in the population7. Under Universal DST the algorithms for diagnosing TB, demonstration of susceptibilities of MDR-TB strains to FQ before initiation of treatment have been incorporated, so that according to DST results the treatment regimen can be changed2,8. With use of nuclei acid amplification test (Xpert MTB/RIF) and probe hybridization techniques (line probe assay), drug resistance are detected early4Culture sensitivity is gold standard and liquid culture (MGIT-960) techniques which have excellent sensitivity and specificity is beneficial when used in high TB burden countries4.

Resistance to FQ is due to mutations in gyr A and gyr B genes which code for enzyme DNA gyrase involved in bacterial DNA replication3,7. FQ resistance among TB patients is due to the use of the drugs for TB as well as for other infections including respiratory as they are broad spectrum, affordable, have high bioavailability, good safety profile and convenient dosing4,7,8. FQ are available over the counter and are regularly prescribed. A retail store audit in India was conducted in 2004 by ORG IMS, reported two highly prescribed antibiotics as ciprofloxacin and Ofx, with gatifloxacin and Lfx being sixth and eighth most frequently prescribed13. FQs are used as first line drugs along with other TB drugs to shorten ATT or as a sequential addition to a failing first-line regimen3. Use of FQ before TB diagnosis was associated with FQ resistance, especially when FQ were used for over 10 days, >60 days ahead of TB diagnosis1. Development of resistance occurs even with very short duration of treatment and within 13 days of exposure to FQ4,8. Studies have reported FQ resistance among drug sensitive TB in India and abroad4,8. FQ resistance is a risk factor for development of XDR-TB.

FQs having significant antimycobacterial activity are Ofx, Lfx, gatifloxacin and Mfx3. Cross resistances among three FQ tested is common7 and was also seen in present study. Cross-resistance within the FQ class is reduced susceptibility to one FQ likely confers reduced susceptibility to all FQ1,7. In this study, 89.8% of MDR-TB isolates resistant to Ofx at base line were also resistant to Lfx and Mfx. Similar results were obtained in studies by Mamatha et al. and Ahmad et al.1,7 Lfx was almost always associated with resistance to other FQs (99%) in the present study. MDR-TB isolates resistant to Ofx and Lfx (13.4%) showed cross-resistance to Mfx 2 μg/mL and hence have an minimum inhibitory concentration (MIC) above that level and hence is not a suitable treatment option.

High resistance above 3 mg/L makes FQ likely to be useless as peak Mfx level in humans is around 3 mg/L3. Resistance to Mfx alone was absent. Absence of resistance to Mfx alone and low crossresistance is supportive evidence for testing of Mfx as candidate for detecting resistance to FQs and also their use in regimens for treatment of MDR-TB. In this study the concentrations of Mfx tested was 2.0 μg/mL as per PMDT guidelines2.Cross-resistance between earlier generation FQ and Mfx is present at lower concentration of 0.25μg/mL3. Mfx is active against strains with low levels of resistance (MIC, 0.5 μg/mL) and reduces mortality on treatment with high dose of Mfx3. With intermediate resistance (MIC, 2.0 μg/ml) it still responds when given along with other second line drugs but has higher relapse rates3,7. The current WHO recommendation is to use Mfx when there is resistance to early-generation FQ, such as Ofx. Superior pharmacokinetic profile of eight methoxy FQ like Mfx makes it a better antimycobacterial and sterilizing agent and thus are used as treatment for MDR-TB with Ofx/Lfx resistance as bacilli may still be susceptible even if cross-resistance is present3. In India FQ resistance is a problem and needs to be addressed by the policy makers urgently so as to control DRTB4. To know the geographical distribution of drug resistant strains, locate their hotspots and related ecological factors in high TB burden countries Shibabaw A et al. proposed the use of geographical information system.

The strengths of this study are large sample size, performance of testing at NTEP/RNTCP certified and quality assured BSL3 laboratory and on all MDR/RR isolates from sputum samples of program defined, presumed RR patients continuously for 1 year from a large geographical area. This reflects situation after implementation of Universal DST which is more realistic and usage of various diagnostic techniques including both conventional and molecular techniques for estimation and confirmation of resistance. Some of the shortcomings of this study are no treatment history and FQ exposure data and no follow up for treatment responses.

In conclusion, in present study MDR-TB/RR TB is 4.1% among all TB patients and additional resistance to FQ among MDR-TB patients was seen in 14.2%. Cross-resistance among FQ was incomplete. Resistance to Mfx alone was absent. Newer generation FQs are promising drugs in the treatment of drug-resistant TB but care should be taken regarding the rationale use of these drugs for the treatment of other diseases especially when other drugs are available. We also support the adoption of a FQ restriction policy in India and also efforts to create awareness among practisingdoctors to use FQ cautiously. Universal DST followed by an individualized regimen based on DST results to control TB in the country is necessary

My topic of interest generated after reading the passage: ______________________________

5Ws and 1 H derived from the passage

My preliminary research question

CHAPTER THIRTY-ONE

Patent filing and Submission

Aim

To understand about patent filing and submission procedure

Introduction

A patent is an exclusive right granted for an invention, which is a product or a process that provides, in general, a new way of doing something, or offers a new technical solution to a problem. To get a patent, technical information about the invention must be disclosed to the public in a patent application. The procedure for granting patents, requirements placed on the patentee, and the extent of the exclusive rights vary widely between countries according to national laws and international agreements. Typically, however, a patent application must include one or more claims that define the scope of protection that is being sought. A patent may include many claims, each of which defines a specific property right. These claims must meet various patentability requirements, which in the US include novelty, usefulness, and non-obviousness (not easily discovered, seen etc.).

A patent, granted by the government, gives an exclusive right to an inventor to make, use, and sell his invention. This exclusive right is for a limited period of 20 years from the date of filing. The fundamental idea is to safeguard the inventions that are created and therefore, encourage more developments.

The Procedure for Patent starts even before an application is filed with the patent office in India.

Procedure

1. Check the patentability of an invention

Before filling a patent application in India, first step is to do a detailed patentability search to determine whether a patent can be granted or not. Your patent should be Novel, Inventiveness (creativity), should have

Industrial Application and Enabling (person skilled in the art should carry out the invention with reasonable practice)

2. Drafting Patent Application

A patent application is filed with the prescribed fee at a patent office in accordance with the jurisdiction. Each patent application is accompanied with patent specification According to the state of invention, you can either file a provisional or complete application. If it is still in development mode it is recommended to file a provisional application to block all important filing dates. A complete specification shall be filed within twelve months from the date of filing of the application, and if the complete specification is not filed, the application shall be deemed to be abandoned. A patent specification should include- Title of the patent invention, Background of the invention, Summary of the invention/ Object of the invention, Explanation if any of the patent drawings, Description of the invention, Patent Claims, Patent Abstract of the disclosure and Sequence listing.

3. Filling the Patent Application

Every application for patent needs to be filed in the forms mentioned below:

Form 1: Application for grant of a patent

Form 2: Provisional/Complete specification

Form 5: Declaration as to inventor ship (only to be filed along with the complete
application)

Form 26: Form for authorization of a patent agent (only required if you are using a
patent agent to help you file the application)

Form 28: To be submitted by startup or small entity (only required if you are claiming
startup or small entity status)

4. Publication of Patent Application

Ever application is published in the official journal after 18th months period from the date of filling of application or the date of priority of application whichever is earlier. There is a provision for early publication of an Indian Patent application by filling a formal request.

5. Examination of Patent Application

Once the application is filed it will end up on the desk of examiner. During examination process examiner will scrutinize application that it is in accordance with Patent Act and Rules. The examiner creates first examination report of the application and will state ground for objections if any. Thereafter the applicant is required to comply with the requirements within a period of 6 months.

6. Grant of Patent

The order of grant is given when all the requirements of patent Act are compiled and it will be published in Patent Journal.

7. Renewal

After the grant of patent, it needs to be renewed from 3rd year onward by paying renewal fee. A Patent in India can be renewed for maximum period of 20 years from the date of filing.

Exercise

Which of the bellow is patentable in India?

1. New Scientific Principle
2. Scientific Principle leading to develop a new machine
3. New bird/animal found
4. Genetically modified organism
5. Human cloning
6. New medical device
7. New medical procedure
8. New form of a known substance
9. Methods in Agriculture
10. A new generator

CHAPTER THIRTY-TWO

Writing Research Proposal

Aim

To understand the components of research proposal and how to write it.

Introduction

A research proposal is intended to convince others that you have a worthwhile research project and that you have the competence and the work-plan to complete it. Generally, a research proposal should contain all the key elements involved in the research process and include sufficient information for the readers to evaluate the proposed study. Regardless of your research area and the methodology you choose, all research proposals must address the following questions: What you plan to accomplish, why you want to do it and how you are going to do it.

Why a good preparation is needed? A good preparation for a research proposal is necessary as: (1) this is vital for grant application in a competitive environment. Funding is very competitive. (2) it assists the researcher in project formulation, planning, performance and monitoring of the research. (3) the quality of the proposal contributes to the evaluation outcome (4) a poorly prepared proposal may not be considered at all or cannot be considered fairly.

Components of a Research Proposal

Title

Introduction

Literature review

Methodology

Plan - time frame and schedule of activities

Budget

Details of research team (signed CV)

Title

The title of a research proposal should be concise and descriptive. Try to think of an informative but catchy title. An effective title not only pricks the reader's interest, but also predisposes him/her favourably towards the proposal.

Introduction

The main purpose of the introduction is to provide the necessary background or context for the research problem. How to frame the research problem is perhaps the biggest problem in proposal writing. The introduction typically begins with a general statement of the problem area, with a focus on a specific research problem, to be followed by the rational or justification for the proposed study.

Objectives of the study

Should be stated clearly

Be clear and concise

Must be measurable and feasible

Literature Review

The aim of the literature review is to provide adequate background information on the research being proposed, especially on: the prevalence or incidence of disease or health problem the current status of selected research topic It should be brief, and indicate relevant related research that had or is being conducted (references should be included). The review committee is normally aware of the various projects going on.

Methodology

The Methodology section is very important because it tells your Research Committee how you plan to tackle your research problem. It will provide your work plan and describe the activities necessary for the completion of your project. For quantitative studies, the method section typically consists of the following sections: Study design -Is it a questionnaire study or a laboratory experiment? What kind of design do you choose (descriptive, cross-sectional, case-control)? Selection of research location Subjects or participants - Who will take part in your study? What kind of sampling method / procedure do you use? You will need to decide on the inclusion and exclusion criteria

Sample size – you need to calculate your sample size based on the type of study you are conducting. There are several formulas for sample size calculation.

Study instruments - What kind of measuring instruments or questionnaires do you use? Why do you choose them? Are they valid and reliable?

Data collection - How do you plan to carry out your study? What activities

are involved? How long does it take?
Data analysis and interpretation – this includes plans for processing and coding data, computer software to be used (eg Statistical Package for Social Sciences / SPSS, EPI-INFO, etc), choice of statistical methods, confidence levels, significance levels etc.
Ethical considerations – It is necessary to submit your research proposal to the Ethical Committee where you work and also where you plan to conduct your research. Depending where you are working and the type of research you are planning to conduct, you are required to submit the Ethical Committee Application Approval Form, together with the research proposal, patient information sheet, patient consent form, etc.

Plan

Planning for the research proposal should include the time frame and activity schedule for the proposed research. The time frame should include time for: purchasing and obtaining relevant consumables and facilities needed to conduct the study conduct of study , analysis of data, writing up of project report
It should list the time frame for major activities, and include milestones. A most effective way of plotting the activity schedule is by using the Gantt Chart

Budget

It is essential to request for an adequate budget for the study you are planning to conduct: Provide a total and yearly breakdown of the budget needed Follow the guidelines provided by the sponsors where you plan on obtaining the grant from Give appropriate estimates of costs depending on the different areas, eg: travel and transportation, consumables, salaries, services, rentals, equipment, utilities, repairs, etc. o Provide adequate justification, especially for costly items

Finally, keep in mind the common errors in proposal writing:
Objectives too broad or too ambitious
Objectives do not reflect title of the study or statement of problem
No literature review or relevant references
Inadequate information on methodology
Inappropriate time-frame and schedule of activities – too ambitious
No justification for Budget – asking for too much or too little

Nomogram For Calculating Rcf For Centrifugation

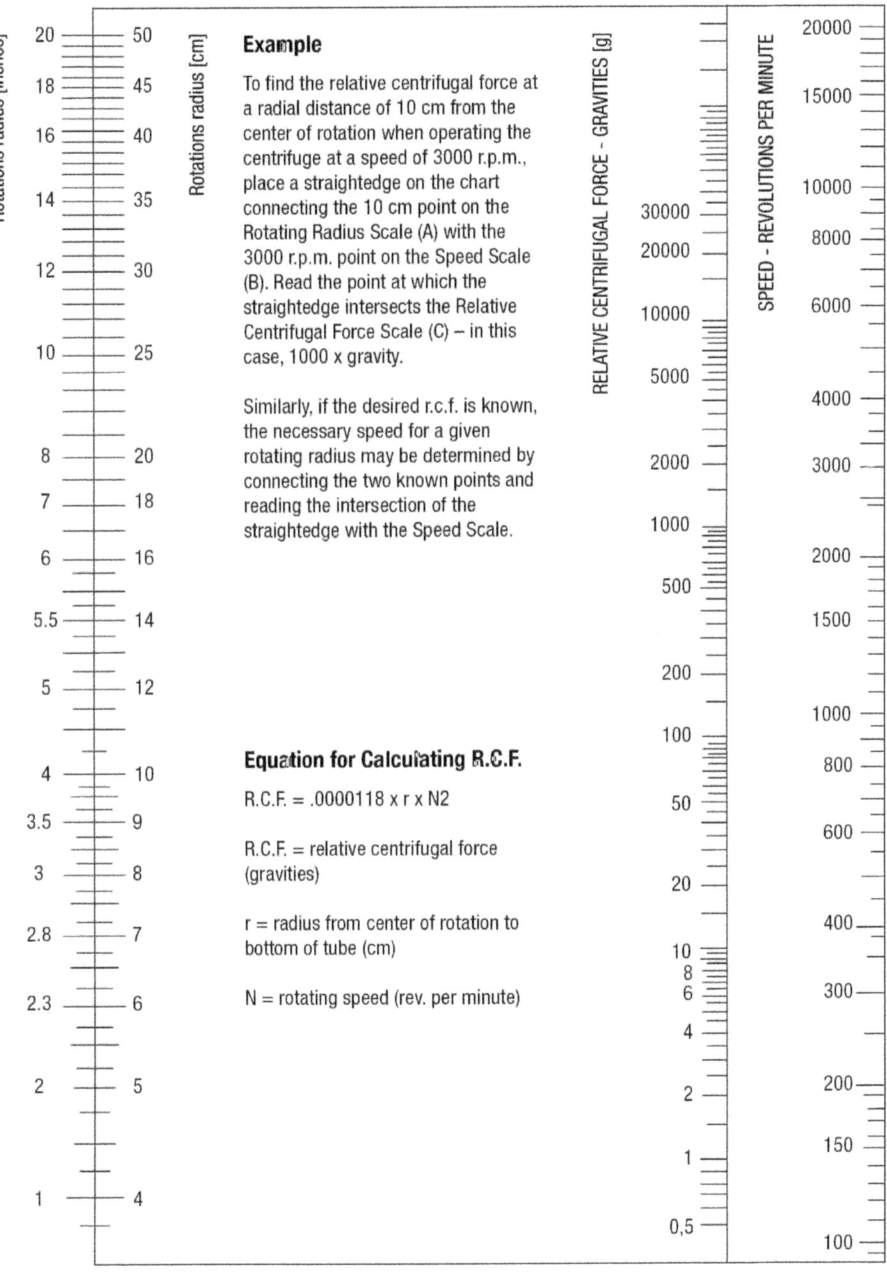

www.ingramcontent.com/pod-product-compliance
Ingram Content Group UK Ltd.
Pitfield, Milton Keynes, MK11 3LW, UK
UKHW022016190726
13853UKWH00005B/1959